Nido Qubein's Professional Selling Techniques

by
Nido R. Qubein

 FARNSWORTH PUBLISHING COMPANY, INC.
Rockville Centre, New York 11570

© 1983 Nido R. Qubein.
All rights reserved.
Published by Farnsworth Publishing Co., Inc.
Rockville Centre, New York 11570.
Library of Congress Catalog Card No. 83-11554.
ISBN 0-910580-78-2.
Manufactured in the United States of America.
No part of this book may be reproduced
without the written permission of the publisher.

Library of Congress Cataloging in Publication Data

Qubein, Nido R.

Nido Qubein's Professional Selling Techniques.

Includes index.
1 Selling.   I. Title   II. Title: Professional selling techniques.
HF5438.25.Q32   1983   658.8'5   83-11554
ISBN 0-910580-78-2

To Mariana,
with love.

Acknowledgements

My gratitude to the hundreds of corporations who engaged me to motivate, educate, and inspire their salespeople ... and to the tens of thousands of individuals who read my books, listened to my cassettes, and attended my seminars. They have all helped me greatly in the development of my career and the enhancement of my work.

I am also very thankful for the love and guidance that I've received through the years from my brothers, Fuad and Ghazi, and from Miss Verta Lawhon, Max H. Cooke, Glenn and Ralph Brown, and other close associates who helped me in the early stages of my life.

To my friend Tom Watson I owe many thanks for the days and nights he spent researching and documenting segments of this book, and much appreciation for his continued advice and encouragement.

To all my colleagues at the National Speakers Association who elected me as their president, to the business and professional leaders who helped me in founding the Nido Qubein Associates Scholarship Fund to educate needy young people, to my partners in the Professional Speakers Group, to my pals in the Furnitureland Rotary Club, to my dedicated office staff, and to my hometown folk in High Point, North Carolina—one big Thank You for believing in me and supporting me so enthusiastically during the last decade.

                                        Nido R. Qubein

About the Author

NIDO R. QUBEIN gives you the formula which has made him one of the most successful salespeople in America, and a trainer of more than 70,000 people each year. *Professional Selling Techniques* grew out of his remarkable rise from the unenviable position of a stranger in a strange land—with little or no money, no connections, and almost no command of the English language—to become one of this country's best-known professional speakers, a very successful businessman, and a highly paid consultant to many of the nation's top business leaders. You'll discover the professional selling techniques that boosted him from virtually no income to assets substantially more than a million dollars in less than 10 years. Nido proves these techniques work by showing you how they have worked successfully for him.

Mr. Qubein now resides in High Point, North Carolina.

Foreword

I'm proud to be called a salesman. I was selling products and services over the air when most "stars" wouldn't even mention their sponsors by name lest their "artistic" talents be tainted by commercialism.

Perhaps that is why my record of 25 years as host of "House Party" and 19 years as the "People Are Funny" star have become landmarks of longevity in broadcasting. I stayed on while others were cancelled because I *"sold."*

I believe Nido has captured the essence of effective selling in this book—I unreservedly recommend it.

Art Linkletter

Contents

Acknowledgements v
Foreword vii
Introduction xi

Chapter

1. Become A Professional Salesperson 7

2. Selling In The New Environment 17

3. Target To Increase Your Effectiveness 33

4. Work Smarter—Not Just Harder 43

5. Beyond Motivation To Mobilization 55

6. Boost Your Selling Brainpower 67

7. Turn What You Know Into What You Can Spend 77

8. Build Your Communication Skills; Boost Your Personal Selling Power 89

9. Ten Ways To Add Power To Your Persuasion . 101

10. Raise Your Customer Response Potential 111

11. Have You Discovered The Power Of Asking Questions? 125

12. Put Power In Your Presentation 137

13. Focus For Maximum Effect 149

14. The Psychology Of Selling 159

15. You Can Become A Master Closer 175

16. Professional Closing Techniques	185
17. Turn Objections Into Sales	197
18. How To Turn Stalls Into Action	211
19. How To Sell Against Competition	221
20. Wanted: Creative Salespeople	235
21. Boost Your Personal Selling Power	251
22. Professional Selling: "Mind Over Matter"	271
Index	275

Introduction

Professional Selling Techniques connects with the most vital element of success in selling all things—yourself! How to sell more in less time and with less effort is the theme of the entire book. In the new selling environment a professional approach, involving professional techniques, is required to sell increasingly sophisticated customers against ever-stronger competition. *Professional Selling Techniques* is a "meaty" book. It is built on the premise that personal selling power comes from what you do and how you do it, rather than how much you do. Concentrated power comes from targeting everything you do to accomplish a specific objective that will move you toward your career goals, and Nido R. Qubein shows you exactly how to do that. Whether you are a beginner or a seasoned veteran, whether you're selling tangibles or intangibles, whether you work on commission or a salary arrangement, you'll find this book enjoyable, helpful, and inspiring.

1.

Become A Professional Salesperson

Join me in a little word-association game that could change your whole outlook on life—and dramatically increase your effectiveness.

If I say to you that a person is a professional person, what's the first word that comes to mind?

Is it doctor? Or lawyer? Or clergyman?

Why is it not salesperson?

I conduct scores of sales training seminars each year throughout this great country of ours, and the most common malady I see is the sales career inferiority complex.

The person who suffers from a sales career inferiority complex usually is hung-up with old, outmoded ideas of what selling is all about. When you say "salesperson," most people think of a back-slapping, joke-telling, fast-talking individual who is always trying to talk somebody into buying something.

I'll let you in on a secret: That approach to selling went out with the dark ages!

Today's effective salesperson is a highly trained, highly skilled, and highly motivated professional person—in the best sense of that word.

It is my goal in this book to help you raise your sights, to help you see yourself as a professional—and to give you information that will help you to become a professional salesperson.

What Makes A Professional?

What do we mean when we say a person is a "professional?" Basically, we mean five things. As I list these five attributes of a professional person, ask yourself if these are not also the five attributes that make a successful *sales*person.

First, a professional person has specialized knowledge and skill that enables him or her to render a valuable service. Do you know many successful salespeople who do not have specialized knowledge and skills?

Secondly, professional people maintain a unique relationship with their clients. People come to them with specific needs and expect them to fulfill those needs. Do not effective salespeople satisfy the needs of their clients with unique products or services? Of course, they do!

Thirdly, professionals render services for which people are willing to pay. You might hit the ceiling when you get your doctor's bill, but when you need treatment you are willing to pay for that service. Effective salespeople can expect to be paid for their services.

Fourthly, professional people are held accountable for the services they render—or fail to render. They are expected to maintain certain standards. Professional salespeople know that they are accountable to the company, to the customers, and to themselves.

The last attribute of professionals is that they have a professional attitude. They know that what they do is vitally important, and seek to do it to the best of their ability. Isn't that a perfect description of the professional salesperson's attitude?

It's this simple! If you are going to be a successful salesperson, you need all of the attributes of a professional. To become a successful salesperson, you must become a *professional* salesperson.

Professionals Get Respect

Rodney Dangerfield has made a fortune expressing the feeling that many salespeople have. He says, "I don't get no respect!"

If salespeople possess all of the attributes of professional people, "How come we don't get no respect?" It's a good question.

Many salespeople do get respect! In most communities in America, some of the top leaders are professional salespeople.

The first step of any professional group in gaining respect from others, is for the people in that profession to respect themselves and what they do, and to respect others who practice their profession.

Professional Problems

"But salespeople have a whole different set of problems than the people we traditionally think of as professionals!" a young woman once said in a sales seminar I was conducting.

I told her that I also have the privilege of speaking to many groups of lawyers, doctors, accountants, and other people we normally think of as professionals. As I have listened to those groups, I have observed that the most common problems they list for their professions are identical to the problems that plague salespeople.

Here's a list of the 10 most common complaints I hear from professional people. I think you will be surprised at how similar they are to problems in sales.

1. The field of their endeavor is changing so rapidly that they have problems keeping abreast of all the new information coming out.

2. They often complain that they are overworked—that they never seem to have enough time to get everything done.

3. The professionals feel that clients often ignore their advice.

4. Their clients often complain that they get paid too much for what they do.

5. Their professional judgments are often criticized by people who know far less than they do about their fields.

6. They feel forced by competition and circumstances to specialize more than they would like to.

7. Many of them had problems getting started in their profession.

8. They often suffer from stress, distress, and burnout.

9. They often feel they are drowning in a sea of detail work, red tape, and paperwork.

10. Their careers often dominate their personal lives.

The professional salesperson encounters every one of these problems!

When I listed those problems for a group of salespeople, one crusty old salesman said, "I know one problem we have that not many doctors and lawyers have. We have to make house calls!"

I had to admit he was right! But, maybe that's offset by the fact that not many salespeople get sued for "malpractice."

In the chapters that follow, I'm going to help you explore how you can apply professional selling techniques to overcome all of the problems we have listed—and others. I'm going to tell you how professional salespeople throughout this country are solving each of those problems and are becoming very successful.

HOW TO BECOME A PROFESSIONAL SALESPERSON

Right now, let's focus on what it takes to become a professional salesperson. How do you develop techniques of professional selling?

For clues, we can go back to the professional attributes I listed earlier and apply them to the selling profession.

ATTRIBUTE #1:
Professional salespeople have specialized knowledge and skills that enable them to render a valuable service to their clients or customers.

Professional salespeople take advantage of every opportunity available to them to learn as much as they can about their business, their products, their companies, their profession, and their competitors.

They study their customers and seek to clearly understand their needs and desires. By understanding those needs and desires, they are able to render valuable services to their customers. The real professional understands what motivates a person to buy—and that is a highly specialized knowledge.

Professional salespeople know their companies and the products and services their companies can provide. They know that often the difference between making or losing a sale is how much they know about what they have to offer their customers. A highly successful salesman once told me, "I pride myself on knowing more about my company and its products than any other person alive!"

There's another thing I've noticed about successful salespeople—they are constantly sharpening their sales skills.

Armed with the knowledge that for today they have mastered all of the specialized knowledge and skills they have had the opportunity to develop, they go out to make their calls with self-confidence.

Professional salespeople believe in their knowledge and skills and only question them in their efforts to hone them to an even keener edge.

ATTRIBUTE #2:
Professional salespeople maintain a unique relationship with their clients, or customers.

They know that their customers rely on them for valuable information which they need to make important decisions; they know their customers expect to be "sold," and they are deeply committed to the customers' best interests. You won't find them begging for an order because they need a commission check, or trying to chisel the customer out of a few extra bucks—and you won't find the professional salesperson being apologetic about his or her enthusiasm.

Professional salespeople value that unique relationship they hold with their clients and seek to establish trust and respect. The real pros in selling build trust through dependable and cheerful service, loyalty, sincerity, and by genuinely protecting the client's interests.

You can always tell the professional salespeople because their customers buy from them again and again, and recommend them to their friends.

ATTRIBUTE #3:
Professional salespeople render a service people are willing to pay for.

Have you heard about the "Weetumpka Grease Factory?" They say it has a great research and development department, an efficient production department, a strong bookkeeping department—but no shipping department! They don't need a shipping department because it takes all of the grease they can manufacture to keep their plant running.

That's the way every plant in America would be operating—or failing to operate—without somebody selling the goods they generate. In fact, someone has said that, "In any business, nothing happens until something is sold."

Sales is such a vital function that most companies are glad to pay commissions and bonuses, or salaries, to get it done. And, most customers recognize that a part of their purchase price goes to pay salespeople.

Professional salespeople have the confidence that they are paid—sometimes very well—for rendering valid services.

ATTRIBUTE #4:

Professional salespeople are accountable, but self-managed.

When a salesperson calls on a customer, that salesperson becomes the official representative of the company. Since the reputation of the company or service organization is on the line with every action by the salesperson, the company feels it has the right to hold them accountable. Most successful salespeople accept reports and expense accounts as "a part of the territory."

They also realize that their integrity is on the line with every report they send in. As one old pro told me, "I never knew anyone that got rich padding an expense account—but I've known a lot of people who got rich by being honest with their company."

Another mark of professionalism in selling is recognizing that the salesperson is accountable to the customer. Those who are really successful don't make false claims, or promises they cannot keep.

Most of all, successful salespeople are self-managed. Their self-respect demands that they work hard, that they show initiative, and that they are persistent. It also demands that they operate ethically and with integrity.

ATTRIBUTE #5:

Professional salespeople have a professional attitude.

Successful salespeople take pride in what they do! They maintain a positive self-image and a strong sense of self-confidence!

They are resourceful in finding prospects, in making presentations, and in solving problems.

They have a sense of responsibility—you can depend on them!

And professional salespeople are open to learn and eager to grow. They are constantly reaching out to tackle new challenges.

The fact that you are reading this book is a strong indication that you have a professional attitude, that you want to be a professional salesperson!

So, what does it take to be a professional salesperson? This quote by B.C. Forbes, the famous magazine publisher, sums it up pretty well. He said, "I once asked 50 of America's foremost men of affairs, 'If you were to name one quality which you regard as the most important, the most valuable, and the most desirable of all in a person, which would you specify?' Next to character, which is all-embracing, courage headed the replies. Loyalty, honesty, and integrity were selected by an equal number, followed closely by intelligence, reliability, industriousness, and judgment."

Those are the marks of a professional salesperson. They provide some valuable clues as to what it takes to be successful in this exciting field we call Professional Selling.

* * *

QUESTIONS FOR REVIEW AND APPLICATION

Rate yourself on a scale of 1-10 on each of the following attributes of a professional person, then set a plan of action for improving in each area:

1. A professional has specialized skills and knowledge that enable him/her to render a valuable service.

MY RATING: (1 2 3 4 5 6 7 8 9 10)

MY PLAN FOR ACTION: _____

2. Professional people maintain a unique relationship with their clients.

MY RATING: (1 2 3 4 5 6 7 8 9 10)

MY PLAN FOR ACTION: _____

_____

3. Professionals render services that people are willing to pay to receive.

MY RATING: (1 2 3 4 5 6 7 8 9 10)

MY PLAN FOR ACTION: _____

_____

4. Professionals are held accountable for the services they render—or fail to render.

MY RATING: (1 2 3 4 5 6 7 8 9 10)

MY PLAN FOR ACTION: _____

_____

5. Professional people have a professional attitude.

MY RATING: (1 2 3 4 5 6 7 8 9 10)

MY PLAN FOR ACTION: _____

_____

2.

Selling In The New Environment

I've always wanted a Mercedes, so one day I just walked into a local showroom to "look around."

Now, there's a little game I like to play on salespeople—I like to make them earn their commission checks. It usually turns out to be a great learning experience for me—and for them.

To set the stage, I walked into that showroom dressed in blue jeans, tennis shoes, and a shirt with several holes in it. It was about 5:30 P.M.

Several salespeople were sitting around talking, and they scarcely glanced up when I came in. Nobody paid any attention to me except a young man.

"Good afternoon, sir," he said with a big smile and an outstretched hand. "My name's John Smith (not his real name). What's yours?"

"Qubein," I muttered as I looked away from him. And I watched to see what would happen.

"I beg your pardon, sir," he said. "Would you repeat your name?"

"Qubein," I replied, taking great care to muffle it even more.

I could tell he was smart because of what he did next.

"Would you spell that for me?" he asked.

As I was spelling my name for him, I overheard one of the other salesmen say, "This boy will someday have to learn how to size up a customer." They all laughed.

"Maybe he'll sell him a bicycle," another chuckled.

What do you suppose his next question was? I was expecting a dumb one like, "Can I help you?" Do you ever feel like saying to a retail salesperson who asks "Can I help you?" something like, "Oh, is this the Salvation Army?" There's another "classic" retail salespeople often use. You walk into a car dealer's showroom, and they say, "You looking for a car?" It always makes me want to say, "No, what I really had in mind was an airplane!" But this guy was different.

"Mr. Qubein," he said in an almost confidential tone, "have you ever owned a Mercedes?"

"Well, no, not really," I replied, and thought to myself, "but thanks for the compliment."

"Let me tell you what's so special about it!" he continued.

That young salesman spent 27 minutes showing and telling me what was "so special" about a Mercedes. He gave me a demonstration ride, showed me a seven-minute audiovisual on the Mercedes, and acquainted me with all the options and color combinations available. He built value on top of value.

"How much?" I asked.

"Mr. Qubein," he said, "for an investment of $40,000 you can discover for yourself what's so special about owning a Mercedes 450SEL!" Then he quickly summarized all the benefits for me.

"That's a lot of money for a car!" I said.

"I agree," he said, "but it's a real good investment because you not only get a Mercedes, your investment will appreciate in value! It's a great hedge against inflation."

"Thanks for your time," I said, "but I'm just looking."

As I started to leave, he asked for my phone number. A couple of days later he called me to set up an appointment to bring over "just the car you said you were looking for—a metallic blue 450SEL Sedan." He showed up right on time. I could tell his sales manager didn't trust him, because he came with him.

Fifteen minutes after they walked into my office, they had a signed order and a check.

"Mr. Qubein," the young salesman said, "you've made a very sound investment!"

"Thank you for helping me make a wise choice," I replied as we headed for the door.

'You know," he said as we were walking out, "there's only one way you could make a better investment."

"How's that?" I asked.

"The only thing you can do to improve this decision is to also get a sports model 450SL that you can ride around in the summer with the top down."

"You find me a metallic gray, with a blue top, and you've sold yourself another car!"

I suspect that he wet his pants right there in my lobby!

Later, as we sat in my office, I asked the sales manager, "When was the last time one of your salesmen sold two cars, worth $80,000, in about 15 minutes?"

"Never!" he answered.

"You may not know this," I continued, "but I spend most of my life training salespeople all over America and in many foreign countries.

"I've got to tell you something," I went on. "There's a big difference in qualifying a customer and sizing one up. If you, and those salesmen who sat around laughing when I walked into your showroom in sneakers, blue jeans, and a ragged shirt, don't know the difference, then may I tell you that the difference is in being a professional salesperson and an amateur—a professional salesperson and an order-taker."

There's a moral to this story, and it is this: The day when you could look a customer over, tell a few jokes, pull out a bag of tricks, and write up an order are long gone—if they ever existed!

In case you have not yet discovered it, the selling situation of today represents a whole new ballgame! People who are going to make a living in this business are going to have to become *professional* salespeople!

CUSTOMERS ARE DIFFERENT

"What's the biggest difference in selling today from when you started out?" I often ask the old pros who attend my seminars.

"The customer is different!" is their almost unanimous reply.

How is the customer different today? Extensive research, and the experience of thousands of successful salespeople, point to at least six significant ways customers are different from those of 30 years ago. Let's look at each and explore what it means to the person who would become a professional salesperson.

CUSTOMER DIFFERENCE #1:
People are busier than ever.

Some of my closest friends and colleagues make a good living, and are constantly in demand. They go all over this country doing nothing but telling people how to make better use of their time.

But you don't need an "expert" to tell you that people are busy. All you need to do is to try to simply drop in on an executive, or a housewife, or a professional person, or even a teenager.

The amateur looks at the "busyness" of people and says, "I've got to work harder to catch anybody, I've got to button-hole everybody I see, and I've got to face the fact that I just can't sell as much as I used to sell."

But the professional salesperson looks at it in a totally different manner. That person knows that the hectic pace of most customers can save him or her time. The professional learns to find and qualify prospects, to spend time with people who have real potential to become customers, to make those precious moments with each customer count, and to reduce lost motion to a bare minimum.

CUSTOMER DIFFERENCE #2:
People have heard it all before.

Selling is the primary function of the private enterprise system which has brought this great country to the highest standard of living in the world. Since World War II there has been a lot of selling going on, and people have heard some of the greatest sales pitches of history from some of the greatest salespeople who have ever lived.

The amateur concludes that people are jaded, that they have heard so many sales presentations they don't want to hear any more.

But the professional takes a different, and more positive view. The sales leaders know that most people expect to be sold—they even want to be sold—that they will make buying decisions if they are sold, and that every presentation must be a major production. They are excited by the challenge, exhilarated by their successes, and educated by their failures.

CUSTOMER DIFFERENCE #3:
People are more "choosey."

The typical customer in almost any product or service category is harder to please than ever before. People want more, for less money; they want better service and less hassle in buying and using what they buy; and they tend to be more vocal when they feel they haven't gotten what they paid for.

Consumers are better educated, more alert, and more aware of what is available. Many have even banded together to form consumer advocacy groups, buying co-ops, and consumer information bureaus.

To the amateur salesperson all this says that it's impossible to please customers anymore. The losers get annoyed at all the complaints, frustrated by those who want to shop around, and discouraged by those who challenge the validity of their claims.

However, the professional salesperson knows that the customer is the most important person in any business. The real producers cash in on the "chooseyness" of customers by making them king or queen of the marketplace. They seek to become knowledgeable about what they are selling and the people to whom they are selling; they look for creative ways to help consumers satisfy their needs and wishes; and they follow up on every sale.

CUSTOMER DIFFERENCE #4:
People are more value-conscious.

Despite all the outcry to the contrary, people have more money to spend now than ever; and some economists predict that our nation's gross national product level will triple during the next decade.

But, at the same time, people are becoming more and more careful as to how they spend that money. If you're out there in the field, you know that you are often the third—or even the tenth—salesperson who has pitched a potential customer. "How much?" comes up much earlier in most presentations, and must be answered much more satisfactorily than ever before.

The loser says that price is the only thing that matters anymore, that customers don't know a bargain when they see one, and that people just don't spend money the way they used to.

"Hogwash!" says the professional salesperson. The winners look at the demands for value as a signal that says, "If you'll show me it's worth your price, I'll buy it!" They set about to build value, to assure the customer he or she is making the right investment and to sell against the competition.

CUSTOMER DIFFERENCE #5:
The typical customer is media-saturated.

It is not unusual for typical young adults to have had more than half-a-million invitations to buy during their first 21 years. They've been promised jobs, girlfriends, boyfriends, sexiness, security, relief from every ailment known to man, and all kinds of feelings. They've been told they're "worth it," they "deserve a break today," and they've been given secrets "your mother never told you."

Today's salespeople have to compete with Cheryl Tiegs, Ricardo Montalban, Robert Young, and a host of well-known athletes and personalities. Customers are geared for glamour, action, and glitter.

Amateurs are discouraged by all the problems brought on by the media. "People listen with one ear and watch with one eye, keeping the other glued to the TV," said one salesperson. "Every 10 minutes they jump up and run out to the bathroom or kitchen." The conclusion: "You can't sell people who won't give you their attention."

But professional salespeople know that gaining and holding attention is their task. They make their presentations an experience for the customer; they involve the customer; and they use the excitement for television and radio as leverage to move the customer to act. The true professional salesperson knows the power of personal contact, and seeks to develop personal power, and the power to be personal with people who live in an impersonal world.

CUSTOMER DIFFERENCE #6:
People are more "self-oriented."

Major emphasis is now being placed on the individual, as opposed to the society. Many people tend to be more independent, more assertive, and more self-centered in their thinking and acting. Buzzwords for the "now generation" are "instant," "self-awareness," "self-fulfillment," and "convenient."

The loser says, "It is impossible to please people anymore!"

But the professional salesperson considers "wish-fulfillment buying" a paradise for creative selling. The professional knows that his or her customers need the salesperson, that they are pleased when you help them make their dreams come true, that they will pay you to help them make up for their weaknesses by satisfying their needs.

The effective salesperson in today's complex marketplace sells ideas, makes ownership a pleasure, and makes the buying decision simple, easy, and convenient.

THE SELLING SITUATION IS DIFFERENT

A highly skilled salesperson from 50 years ago dropped suddenly into the selling situation of today would be as confused as Rip Van Winkle, who had slept through the American Revolution. His or her attempts to communicate with a prospect would probably be just as ineffective as were those of old Rip in trying to reach the Colonists with his "God save the king!"

The professional salesperson knows that the marketplace has changed—and keeps changing—and keeps reaching out to stay abreast of what those changes mean. The real professional is like the doctor who studies the latest medical bulletins, and the attorney who keeps up with current legislation in his or her area of specialization.

Let's consider some of the obvious changes that are taking place in the selling situation, and what those changes mean for the person who wants to be an effective salesperson.

SELLING SITUATION CHANGE #1:
Costs of selling are increasing rapidly.

Every call we make becomes a major investment—both to the salesperson and his or her company. Travel costs, entertainment costs, materials and sample costs, and administrative costs seem to spiral upward every month.

The salesperson of a generation ago might have been able to rely on an occasional friendly visit with a customer, just to keep the lines of communication open. But a "chitchat" call is rapidly becoming a thing of the past. It simply costs too much (and takes up too much time) to make aimless calls.

Effective selling now involves careful planning, targeting of resources for maximum effect, and a much more skillful use of the telephone and other communication aids.

SELLING SITUATION CHANGE #2:
Travel is more complex.

The speed of travel has increased so much that it's possible to breakfast with a client in New York, have lunch with another client in Chicago, and eat dinner with a third client in San Francisco. But as travel has speeded up, it has also become much more complex. Parking, finding accessible hotel rooms, meshing schedules, and transporting materials grow increasingly complex every day.

Knowledge of the territory, careful planning of schedules, setting up advance appointments, and maximizing selling time is as much a part of being an effective salesperson in today's complex marketplace as is the actual process of selling.

"What's the greatest challenge you face in selling?" I once asked an old pro.

Without hesitation he replied: "Being at the right place, at the right time, with the right people, and doing the right thing at all times!"

SELLING SITUATION CHANGE #3:
There are more specifiers and professional buyers.

A salesperson who has been calling on the president of a company for years, often finds that he or she is suddenly required to work with a buyer, a purchasing agent, or a specifier. An automobile dealer told me recently that he was amazed at how many consumers had called him during the last year and asked him to submit a sealed bid on an automobile they had specified.

The more sophisticated buyers become, the more new skills the salesperson who wants to continue to be effective must learn. It means we must develop more effective methods of getting to the decision-makers, greater adaptability to changing buying patterns, and more creative approaches to our presentations.

SELLING SITUATION CHANGE #4:
Customers demand more information.

A salesperson who relies on a "good snow job" with many of today's educated consumers and professional buyers is likely to go hungry. Many customers want very specific information about any product or service they are considering purchasing.

Add to that the fact that more and more information is available to the salesperson, from a wider variety of sources, and it means that the effective salesperson must be an avid reader, a sharp listener, and a keen observer.

SELLING SITUATION CHANGE #5:
Competition is becoming increasingly sophisticated.

"Show me a better mousetrap today, and tomorrow I'll show you a dozen versions of it that are better, cheaper, and more convenient to obtain," someone said recently.

As the marketplace grows tighter and tighter, competitors become more and more sophisticated with their sales aids, their marketing approaches, and their service systems. The professional salesperson knows that keeping abreast of the competition is a must.

"Send me a salesperson who can think, who can be creative in selling, who can outperform the competition," a sales manager told me recently.

SELLING SITUATION CHANGE #6:
The pace of life has quickened.

People move more often, change jobs more often, and their incomes fluctuate more wildly than ever before. New corporate customers spring up overnight, steady accounts of long-standing suddenly go out of business, and people get married—or divorced—and corporations merge.

The professional salesperson knows that only those who can keep up with the pace, can adjust and adapt to changing situations most effectively, and can see the opportunities brought about with the changes, can stay ahead of the game.

SELLING SITUATION CHANGE #7:
National and local economies grow increasingly complex.

Many potential customers are finding it less and less convenient to buy things. One year the predominant problem is inflation, the next year it's tight money, another year it's high interest rates, and the next year it's a combination of those factors plus a host of others.

The creative salesperson who can help customers wade through all of the systems, economic factors, and red tape to make purchasing easy and convenient, is very much in demand in today's complex market.

THE NEW PROFESSIONAL SALESPERSON

A highly successful dentist in High Point, North Carolina, where I live, recently told me: "In dental school they taught me how to treat dental problems and foster dental health, but they taught me nothing about maintaining good patient relationships, or supervising staff people, or managing money—and those areas are where I spend most of my time."

I told him that many of the salespeople I work with in audiences across America are finding that they have a similar situation. They are finding that there is a lot more to being an effective salesperson than simply making calls, telling their sales story, and writing up orders.

* * *

APPLICATION AND REVIEW

Here is a list of some of the skills and disciplines of the new professional salesperson who is effective in the changing selling situation. Rate yourself on a scale of 1 to 10 on each of the skills or disciplines described below, and set a goal for improving in each area.

1. An ability to set realistic goals and follow those goals through to a satisfactory completion—the ability to make things happen.

(1 2 3 4 5 6 7 8 9 10)

2. An ability to communicate effectively—to convey a message that produces a desired response.

(1 2 3 4 5 6 7 8 9 10)

3. An ability to manage resources, opportunities, and difficulties in a way that produces the greatest return.

(1 2 3 4 5 6 7 8 9 10)

4. A self-discipline that makes every minute count for maximum return.

(1 2 3 4 5 6 7 8 9 10)

5. A working knowledge of the selling process, of their products and services, of their companies and industries, and the wisdom to know how to effectively utilize that knowledge.

(1 2 3 4 5 6 7 8 9 10)

6. A pleasing, enthusiastic, and forceful personality.

(1 2 3 4 5 6 7 8 9 10)

7. An ability to turn each presentation into a major production.

(1 2 3 4 5 6 7 8 9 10)

8. A willingness to ask questions, to listen to responses, and to observe everything the customer does.

(1 2 3 4 5 6 7 8 9 10)

9. A working knowledge of closing techniques, and a skill in choosing and using the right one for each situation.

(1 2 3 4 5 6 7 8 9 10)

10. An ability to turn objections into sales and stalls into action.

   (1 2 3 4 5 6 7 8 9 10)

11. The character and integrity to build trusting relationships.

   (1 2 3 4 5 6 7 8 9 10)

12. The patience, persistence, and concern for the customer's best interests.

   (1 2 3 4 5 6 7 8 9 10)

We will look at each one of these skills and disciplines in depth in the chapters that follow.

3.

Target To Increase Your Effectiveness

"Sir, I want a raise!" the salesperson said firmly. He went on to point out that he had been with the company for a year and that he had worked very hard.

"Very well," replied the boss, "I'll put you on straight commission. . . . Your raise will become effective when you become effective!"

Webster gives two definitions of the verb "effect." They are "to accomplish" and "to produce." I don't know of any two words that describe better what the salesperson is expected to do! It is these two results or actions that make salespeople effective.

And what does "effective" mean? In the dictionary, you'll find three powerful descriptions of what it means to be effective as a salesperson. Successful salespeople are "producing a decided effect," they are "ready for service or action," and they are "strikingly impressive."

You didn't know you were going to get a grammar lesson, did you? But, sometimes it is helpful to take words that we throw around like fertilizer and zero-in on exactly what they mean to us.

Are you an effective salesperson? Or, as a sales manager I know at an industrial company I consult with often asks applicants for sales positions, "Do you make sales, or do you make excuses?"

Effective, professional salespeople are some of the most exciting people I know!

How Effective Are You?

One thing that makes them exciting is that they love a challenge—they are always open to new possibilities!

Here are some challenging questions for you! Are you as effective as you want to be? Would you like to increase your effectiveness, and your income?

If you would like to become more professional by becoming more effective, I will tell you in this chapter exactly how to do it!

I know that salespeople can be a little skeptical by nature, so I'll get right to the bottom line. *If you want to increase your effectiveness, make a solid commitment to targeting!*

When I say target, what's the first image that comes to your mind? *BULLSEYE! You've got it!*

A target is a mark to shoot at—a goal to be achieved.

I once heard about a kid who was going into a golden gloves boxing match. "Keep your chin up, keep your hands up, he won't lay a glove on you!" his coach told him before the fight.

The bell rang, the kid went out, and the other kid just pulverized him!

"Keep your chin up, keep your hands up, he didn't lay a glove on you!" the coach said at the end of the first round.

Second round, same story!

By the end of the third round the kid was blurry-eyed and rubber-kneed.

"You're doin' great, kid," said the coach. "He hasn't laid a glove on you yet!"

"Then, you'd better watch that referee, coach," said the kid. "Somebody out there's beatin' the heck out of me!"

That story always reminds me of many salespeople I've seen around the hotels where I stay. Believe me, you can hear some interesting things through hotel walls.

One side of a telephone conversation I heard at the St. Francis Hotel in San Francisco a few weeks ago was so potent that I only needed to hear one side of it. It went like this:

"No, I didn't get to see him."

"No, him either."

"He wasn't in—but I talked with his assistant."

"No!"

"Four."

"Whadda' you mean only four. . . . Do you know what kind of a day I've had?"

There was a long silence, then the voice loudly quoted a line from a popular Johnny Paycheck song. . . . It was something about what the person on the other end of the line could do with his job.

Have you ever felt like that guy? He felt he had done the best he could have done, that he had been up against insurmountable odds, and that somebody out there had "beaten the heck out of him!"

He had never learned the power of targeting!

Coach Paul "Bear" Bryant, who won more football games than any coach in the history of college football, offered this simple formula for winning. "First, you've got to keep the other team from scoring more points than you do, and second, you've got to score more points than they do."

If you want to be a successful salesperson, you've got to keep the other team from scoring more points than you do. Who is the other team? They have names like "never enough time," and "people are too busy," and "too much competition," and "bad economic conditions."

How do you score more points than that team of monsters? You get more orders than they take away from you!

Targeting—setting goals and objectives—is your best bet for increasing your effectiveness—and your income!

WHY TARGET?

Why should you set goals? I'll give you 10 good reasons:

1. Goals give you something to work for. They give purpose and direction to your life. Desire is the key to all self-discipline. If what you're working for really matters, you'll give it all you've got.

2. Goals give you the best reason in the world for not procrastinating.

3. Goals help you to concentrate all of your energies and resources in a specific direction. They help you focus the full power of your abilities—and that's a lot of power!

4. Goals help you build enthusiasm! They help you to get excited and excite others.

5. Goals help you be specific with other people. If you ask people to do something in a general way, that's the way they'll do it. Ask them to do something specific, in a given time, and you'll get it done.

6. Goals help you save time for yourself, your clients, and everyone else in your life.

7. Goals save you money, and make you money.

8. Goals help you keep in perspective what's really important so you don't spend all of your time doing what seems urgent.

9. Goals give you a standard against which you can measure your effectiveness. You can reward yourself when you reach your goals, and learn from your failures when you don't reach them.

10. Goals provide an excellent foundation for setting new targets at which you want to aim.

Some of the best advice I ever received was, "If you would be successful, study the lives of successful people, and try to do exactly what they have done."

I have read the biographies of many of the greatest people who ever lived and made an interesting discovery—*they all knew where they were going—they all had targets they were aiming at.*

HOW SHOULD YOU SET GOALS?

Targets only have meaning when they produce tangible results in the laboratory of life. Here are seven guidelines that can help you set targets you can hit—goals you can reach:

1. *Set goals that are consistent with your purpose in life!* One way to determine your purpose in life is to write down what you want most out of life. You might be surprised! For example, many people say what they want most is to become very, very rich. Yet, if you were to suggest they join the "Mafia," you'd find out quickly that money is not the most important thing in their lives. Choose goals that reflect your values, your purpose in life.

2. *Set goals that you can get excited about!* One reason many salespeople fail to meet their quotas is that those are goals somebody else has set for them. What excites you? A new home? A vacation in the Bahamas? A promotion? Set goals you can become enthusiastic about. Remember, the key to self-discipline is desire.

3. *Set goals that meet your needs as a total person!* It is possible to maintain a balanced life and be very successful. For example, some of the most successful salespeople I know have very good family relationships, are thoroughly committed to their churches, and are very active in their communities. In addition, they still have time to pursue hobbies. They have learned to set goals in all areas of their lives.

4. *Set goals that are high enough to deserve your very best, but not too high to be reachable!* Someone has

said that it is better to aim too high and miss than to aim too low and hit your target. Robert Browning, the romantic poet, said, "Ah, but a man's reach should exceed his grasp, or what's a heaven for?" I would bet that such a person is going to need a heaven, because that person is going to spend his life in frustration. Only you can decide what goals are high enough for you, but I would suggest somewhere between "aiming too low" and "exceeding your grasp."

5. *Set goals that are specific and measurable.* The person who says, "I'm going to make as many sales as I possibly can," will find that goal hard to keep in focus. But the person who says, "I'm going to increase my sales by 10 percent each year," and does it, will double his or her sales in just seven years. The person who targets to read three books per month, will read 36 books each year, while the person who targets to "read everything I can get my hands on," is not likely to read nearly that many. Be specific—set measurable goals!

6. *Write down your goals!* Remember the old eastern proverb? It says, "The palest ink is stronger than the most enduring memory." Salespeople who've been selling for years know that you cannot count a sale until you receive the signed order! Your goals are a promise, a commitment you make to yourself and other people who matter to you. Take them seriously —just like you would a contract. You might even want to draw them up in the form of a contract, date it, and sign it. Once you have written your goals down, keep them where you can read them often to help you keep them clearly in focus.

7. *Set deadlines for your goals!* One good way to do that is to set three types of goals: Long range, intermediate range, and immediate targets.

Long-range goals will give you direction for five to ten years.

Intermediate-range goals will move you toward your long-range goals and help you accomplish things that won't require that much time. They should be for one to three years.

Immediate goals will give you the step-by-step objectives you need to start the journey to your long-range goals. They should cover three months to one year.

GOALS: THE WINNER'S EDGE

Do you remember that challenge I gave to you early in this chapter? I said, "If you want to increase your effectiveness, make a solid commitment to targeting!"

Your goals are only as helpful as your commitment to them is strong.

Have you ever noticed the times of Olympic races of various kinds? Most of them are won by a few hundredths of a second, even though the event might last for more than an hour. The winners are not superhuman! *They are just a little bit better than their competition! But it is that slight edge that gives them their secret of success!*

Some of those athletes train for years—they practice and practice and practice—for an event that may take only a few minutes. And then they win only by a slim margin. But, if you study their training programs, you'll find that all of them have made a practice of setting goals and reaching the goals they set.

For every gold medal winner, there are thousands of people who started out to reach that goal. *Setting realistic goals, and meeting those goals, is the winner's competitive edge.*

Most of us will never have a target that is as vital as that famous William Tell target. He's the fellow who had to put the apple on his little boy's head and shoot through it with his bow and arrow. If that kid had hiccupped, he would have had a permanent part in his hair—and William Tell would have been listed in history as a villain, instead of a hero.

But salespeople who consistently set their next goal somewhat, but not too much, above their last achievement and consider all of their targets as vitally important become increasingly effective.

If we may go back to Webster—*they become strikingly impressive!*

* * *

GROWTH EXERCISE

List three specific ways goals have helped you become more effective:

1. _____
_____
_____
_____

2. _____
_____
_____
_____

3. _____
_____
_____
_____

EVALUATE YOUR GOALS

Here are seven guidelines for setting goals. If you do not have clear goals, use the guidelines to set goals. If you already have goals, check the appropriate column at the right and see the rating scale at the bottom of the page.

Goal-Setting Guidelines	Good	Needs Improvement	Poor
1. Set goals that are consistent with your purpose in life.			
2. Set goals you can get excited about.			
3. Set goals that meet your needs as a total person.			
4. Set goals that are high enough to deserve your very best, but not too high to be unreachable.			
5. Set goals that are specific and measurable.			
6. Write your goals down and refer often to them.			
7. Set guidelines for each of your goals.			
TOTAL			

RATING SCALE: Score yourself as follows: 10 points for each "good" check, 5 for each "needs improvement," and 0 for each "poor" answer.

NOTE: If you scored yourself 60 or more, you are probably well on your way to reaching your goals. A score of 45-60 means you can boost your effectiveness a great deal by refining goals. A score of 40 or less means you have many exciting things to discover about goals.

4.

Work Smarter— Not Just Harder

When a salesperson says to me, "I sold more last year than anyone has ever sold in my territory," I say, "That's great! But, let me ask you a question—Are you selling *all* that you can sell in your territory?"

It is important to measure your performance against your past successes, but it is even more important to measure your performance against your *potential*.

"I'm working as *hard* as I can," you say.

But are you working as smart as you can? That is the key question!

Earl Nightengale says that most people who work themselves to death die poor. It is that person who works *smart* that becomes rich.

The secret of building the value of your assets is to invest those assets in the way that brings the greatest possible return.

As a salesperson you have two great assets to invest—your time and your talents. The more wisely you invest them in your career, the greater the return you will receive from them.

I have met many people who had great talents—they were effective communicators, they were very persuasive—but they were lousy salespeople! Why? Because they wasted their most valuable commodity—*time*!

They didn't want to waste time; they were always busy; but time just seemed to slip through their fingers.

If you would learn just three things that could help you save several hours each week, the time you spend reading this chapter would be very wisely invested. Don't you agree?

MAKE TIME WORK FOR YOU—NOT AGAINST YOU

If you would like to turn your territory into a goldmine, you need all of the dexterity of a professional juggler. A professional juggler can keep half a dozen balls in the air, while balancing an expensive piece of crystal on a bowling pin on his or her head. And make it look so *easy!*

How do they do it? They have mastered the art of keeping several things going at once, through *scheduling*. They have developed the skill of *timing!*

To the professional salesperson, timing means these things: time management through territory planning which leads to opportunity management. Master those things, and you can turn your territory into a goldmine.

Do you manage your time, or does your time manage *you?* There's a surefire way to find out. Just ask yourself if you never seem to have enough time to get done all the things you *want* to get done. Do you often say, "If I just had *more* time..."?

I have good news and I have bad news for you! First, the bad news—there isn't any more time. There are only 60 minutes in each hour, 24 hours in each day, and seven days in each week; and nobody can do *anything* about that!

Now for the *good* news—You don't *need* any more time! You'll find that time can work to your advantage when you manage it wisely.

It is important to decide on your objectives, and to create a schedule that will allow you to meet those objectives in the *shortest* amount of time. Manage your time through organization and planning.

TIME-MANAGEMENT TIPS

Here are some tips to help you:

TIP #1—Put yourself on a schedule!

Did you ever see the sign that says, "The hurrier I go the behinder I get"? That's the mark of an unscheduled person.

Be your own clock. Make your daily routine fit into a time pattern that will utilize your waking hours to the utmost. A fixed schedule is one of the best time management tools ever devised. It is the only way to effectively minimize lost motion and interruptions.

TIP #2—Organize your presentations!

Don't waste time fumbling for the right words. Professionals know what they want to say, and they say it in the least amount of words and in the least amount of time.

Also, know your customer's potential so that you can budget *more* time with likely "big spenders" and *less* time with little spenders. Make it your business to know your customer's needs *before* you begin your presentation.

TIP #3—Build in flexibility!

Delayed or cancelled appointments are sometimes unavoidable, but you can turn that limbo time into *productive* time in several ways. If you know the delay will last more than 15 minutes, leave a polite note saying you will schedule another appointment. If you must wait, go back over your presentation, or read company reports or letters, or select a passage from your scheduled reading list—not from the old magazines on the table in the waiting area.

TIP #4—Make travel time work for you!

Always map out your complete travel plans on paper—*before you leave!* Look for the shortest routes and schedule appointments in the same area close together. When you're on a train, bus, or plane, use this time to read or do paperwork.

If you get tied up in traffic, don't fuss and fume the time away. Listen to a cassette, or critique your last presentation.

TIP #5—Get yourself organized!

Organize your desk, your car, your office—even your luggage—so that you won't spend valuable time searching for important materials. Keep samples and catalogs neatly stored for easy access. Don't be a paper shuffler—be a paper *processor.*

TIP #6—Keep a daily "to do" list!

Write down those little things you must get done between appointments—and then do them!

If you try to remember all of the things you *should* do, you not only will overlook some important things, you will find that carrying all of that around in your memory can sap your energy and affect your concentration. Always know what you're going to do next.

When you encounter a delay, just look down your "to do" list and select the most important item—and *do* it.

TIP #7—Watch your attitude!

When you say, "I was in the area, so I thought I'd just drop in," what you are *really* saying is, "My time is not *really* important." Perhaps even worse, you are saying to your customer, "*Your* time is not important."

TIP #8—Seek good appointments!

What makes a good appointment?

First, a good appointment is at a convenient *time* for the prospect and the salesperson.

Secondly, a good appointment is at a convenient *place* for all concerned.

Thirdly, an appointment is only good when a *decision-maker* is present.

Finally, a good appointment is when you are *prepared* to make your *best* presentation.

Of course, I know that sometimes a good appointment is one that you can *get*. But, when you gain the reputation as one who always says, "*My* time is *your* time," you can easily become a slave instead of a professional salesperson.

Let me ask you a question. Would you say to a client, "My money is your money"? It is more true of salespeople than of any other professional, that *your time* is *your money!*

TIP #9—Guard your action time!

The television industry has coined the term "*prime time.*" It is that time, in the evenings, when they have the largest potential audience of the day. If you want to buy a spot in prime time, you will pay dearly for it—because it is the most valuable time they have to sell! Your "prime time," or "*action* time," is the time you actually spend in the presence of qualified buyers. There are two important principles to keep in mind about action time.

First, make it count! Don't waste a precious second of a precious minute. Move the client toward your goal as quickly as possible, without making that client feel rushed or pressured.

Secondly, always work toward increasing your action time! You can do that in several ways:

—Improve your sales call scheduling and planning.

—Handle service calls by phone, and do as much selling by phone as you can.

—Use waiting time as productively as you can.

TIP #10—Guard against bad habits that waste time!

Keep a constant vigil against habits like:

—Leaving your home, office, or motel *late*.

—Making several return calls on *poor* prospects.

—Making too many *social* calls on good accounts.

—Ignoring the fact that many of your prospects are in their offices *before* nine, *after* five, and on Saturdays and Sundays.

—Spending three hours of potential action time to take an old friend to lunch.

—Not imposing self-discipline.

These bad habits are *all* time wasters!

TIP #11—Put off procrastination!

I have seen many salespeople who put burglar alarms on their cars, in their luggage, on motel doors, on their homes—anywhere they think a robber might seek to steal something that is valuable from them. Yet, many of those same salespeople pay no attention to the most clever thief of all—*procrastination!*

"I need to call on that prospect, *one* of these days. . . ."
"I've got to settle that customer's complaint, *soon*. . . ."
"I've got to update my samples and catalogs, as soon as I get around to it. . . ." And on, and on it goes!

Somehow we kid ourselves into believing that we will have more time, at a later date. Or, we convince ourselves that an unpleasant task will become more pleasant, if we put it off. Yet, there never seems to be a more convenient time, and usually, the unpleasant task becomes even more unpleasant the longer we put it off.

Someone said, "You don't judge a person by what that person *starts*; you judge that person by what he or she *finishes.*"

If a task is worth doing, it is worth doing at the earliest reasonable time. If it is not worth doing, *forget* it!

Do you want to know how to conquer procrastination? Put teeth into your schedule by setting deadlines for everything you do.

When something you need to do comes to mind, do it immediately if that seems the most logical thing to do. If not, write into your schedule a specific time that you will have it done by—then *do* it *before* that time rolls around.

Procrastination is a thief which robs you of money by stealing your time, which robs you of self-respect and the respect of others, and saps some of your most creative energies. Be a crimestopper—*Stop procrastinating!*

TIP #12—Make time-saving a positive, daily habit!

For the professional salesperson, time management is a way of life!

Don't let the clock bully you! Learn to be a businesslike person. Time-wasters become slaves to the clock. They rush around like crazy trying to get everything done. They are usually not lazy; they just don't manage their time wisely. They let their time manage *them* unwisely!

TIME SAVED IS MONEY EARNED

Do you remember the good news and the bad news I gave you early in this chapter? The bad news was that you were not going to get any more time. But the good news was that you didn't *need* any more time.

Time-wasting is a nasty habit that grows up on its own. It is like a weed in a garden. It just grows and grows without any encouragement from you.

But time-saving is a habit you can cultivate. It is the only way you can really take charge of your life, that you can be your own boss.

Want to turn your territory into a goldmine? Study and practice these 12 tips for practical time management. To paraphrase Ben Franklin: An hour saved is money earned—and you can take that to the bank!

What's it worth to you to save one single hour every day? In a normal lifetime, one hour saved each and every day of a five-day week is worth *six years* of productive effort.

What does that mean in terms of money? Of course, it depends on how much you make, but, based on a normal workweek, you can figure out exactly how much money an hour saved can mean to you.

The following chart will give you some idea as to how much you can save. It is based on 244 workdays of eight hours each, excluding breaks.

Annual Income	Each Hour Is Worth	Each Minute Is Worth	In a Year an Hour Per Day Saved Is Worth
$ 10,000	$ 5.16	$ .0864	$ 1,259
12,000	6.16	.1024	1,503
14,000	7.16	.1192	1,748
16,000	8.16	.1360	1,992
20,000	10.32	.1728	2,518
25,000	12.81	.2134	3,125
30,000	15.37	.2561	3,750
35,000	17.93	.2988	4,375
40,000	20.64	.3596	5,036
50,000	25.62	.4268	6,250
75,000	38.42	.6403	9,374
100,000	51.24	.8536	12,500
125,000	64.03	1.067	15,623
150,000	76.84	1.280	18,749
175,000	89.65	1.494	21,875
200,000	102.45	1.707	24,998

* * *

TAKE ACTION TO SAVE TIME

In this chapter, we gave you 12 tips to help you work smarter. The time to start using them is now! After you review each tip, set a specific goal for improving in that area:

1. Put yourself on a schedule.
GOAL: _____

2. Organize your presentations.
GOAL: _____
_____

3. Build in flexibility.
GOAL: _____
_____

4. Make travel time work for you.
GOAL: _____
_____

5. Get yourself organized.
GOAL: _____
_____

6. Keep a daily "to do" list.
GOAL: _____
_____

7. Watch your attitude toward time.
GOAL: _____
_____

8. Seek good appointments.
GOAL: _____
_____

9. Guard your action time—the time you spend before prospects selling.
GOAL: _____
_____

10. Guard against bad habits that waste time.
GOAL: _____
_____

11. Put off procrastination.
GOAL: _____
_____

12. Make time-saving a daily habit.
GOAL: _____
_____

5.

Beyond Motivation To Mobilization

"I come to a motivational session like this, or read an inspiring book, and get all excited about making the most of my opportunities," said a young woman after a seminar I had just conducted.

"Then," she continued, "I go back to my territory and work like crazy for about a week. . . . Then I get discouraged because nothing is happening.

"It's getting harder and harder to kick myself enough to get me going," she concluded.

"You'd say you're pretty frustrated?" I asked.

"That's putting it mildly!" she said.

I shared with that young saleswoman a secret I learned early in my sales career that has made my work not only more productive, but a constant joy. The secret is this: *Motivation without mobilization means only frustration!*

The primary difference between an amateur salesperson and a professional salesperson is that the amateur is always looking for a better territory, or a better product, while the professional is always looking for a better way to work with what he or she has been given.

Lack of motivation is indeed a problem for many salespeople. Desire, after all, is the key to all self-discipline. Nothing works unless you do!

However, even the greatest motivators in history have all indicated that it is impossible to continually motivate yourself without turning that motivation into rewarding results.

To make motivation pay off, it is necessary to mobilize all of your resources in the direction of your goals.

Professional salespeople get more done in less time, and have time left over to enjoy life because they live by one simple credo: "Manage your work, don't let it manage you!"

They decide what they want from their territories, rather than waiting for their territories to make demands from them. They don't wait for things to happen—they make things happen!

Would you like your territory to become more productive? Would you like to make more sales, and more commissions, with less effort? And, would you like to have time enough to spend with your family, on hobbies, and just doing things you like to do? It's possible for you to do just that! In fact, I know many salespeople who are doing it right now.

The following six steps are the steps they have taken, and continue to take:

STEP #1—Become a territorial goal setter!

Manage your territory by targeting—by zeroing in on the things you want to accomplish!

We talked about setting goals in your personal life. Now we are talking about setting goals in your professional life.

What's the best way to set a long-range goal for your territory?

Sit down with a pencil and a piece of paper and ask yourself some tough questions.

Question #1: "What would I like my territory to look like five years from now?" How many units would you like to be selling each year? How many customers would you like to be calling on each week? How much time would you like to be putting into your work?

Question #2: "Are my ambitions for my territory realistic?" Don't undersell your abilities. Let's say you want to double your sales within the next five years. If you can increase your sales by 15% each and every year for the next five years, you can *double* your *present volume.* Make sure that the goals you set are measurable. Think in terms of percentage of increase in *units* sold. Dollar volume increases are unreliable because of inflation.

If you sold a million dollars worth of goods or services last year, and raised that to a million and one hundred thousand this year, all you did was break even. Inflation gave you a 10% increase. It also gave you a 10% increase in expenses—at least!

Question #3: "What would be the benefits to me from achieving this goal?" There is only one person in the world who can motivate you to reach your territorial goals, and that is you! If it is not worth the effort, in terms of benefits you will receive, you are wasting your time and paper to write the goal down.

Now, write your goal down with a specific target date for reaching it. Once you develop the habit of goal setting, you'll not only be hooked for life, you'll look for ways to use goals in everything you do. You'll find yourself setting goals for each of your accounts, for every day of your life; even for building family relationships. Why? Because you will discover *it works!*

STEP #2—Manage your territory by objectives!

The most important question in setting objectives is: "What do I have to *do* to make my goals become reality?"

There are only two ways to increase your sales. Horizontally and vertically! When you increase sales horizontally, you increase the number of customers you have. This is a good way to make your territory *grow,* but it is also a good way to increase your expenditures of money, effort, and time.

When you increase sales vertically, you increase the volume of sales by selling more to the customers you now *have.* This is often the most productive area of concentration because it gives the greatest return on your investment, and affords opportunities for future growth.

Now you are ready for . . .

STEP #3: Plan your strategies to meet your goals and objectives!

Here the most important question is: "How do I go about meeting my objectives?"

If one of your objectives is to increase sales by selling more to fewer customers, a good strategy would be to spend more time cultivating those customers that have the most po-

Beyond Motivation To Mobilization

tential. Take a cold, hard look at the time you devote to *each* account. Don't be surprised if you discover that you spend 80% of your time with those accounts that produce only 20% of your volume.

Many professionals classify their customers in three categories:

—Their *"A"* accounts are their bread and butter customers—the ones who account for *most* of their sales. And, here's where they spend most of their time.

—Their *"B"* customers produce small volume but have *potential.* Therefore, they get less attention, but are still important.

—*"C"* customers and prospects produce small volume and have little potential for growth, so they get the *least* amount of time.

The principle is like farming—plant the most seeds in the most fertile ground.

Always balance your strategies against *all* of your objectives. For example, let's say one of your objectives is to increase your action time by reducing travel time, while another might be to concentrate more time on *key* accounts. Then it makes sense to spend some time developing prospects that have potential in those far-off areas where you only have one or two accounts.

Ever watch a professional *pool* player? He studies every move carefully *before he makes it!* An amateur might say, "That's an easy shot . . . go ahead and make it." But the pro has something else in mind. He's planning how he will use *this* shot to *set up* the *next* one!

That's the key to *managing* your territory—Planning *every* move so that it contributes to the objectives that will take you to your goals.

"But, I don't have time for that junk," a harried salesperson said to me. "I've got too much work to do!" I would bet you that five years from now that salesperson will still be harried, still be barely making a living, and still be complaining about the territory.

The choice is yours! You can either work yourself to death trying to make sales, or you can plan to manage your opportunities and turn your territory into a goldmine.

STEP #4—Schedule your work!

The key question here is: "How do I spend my time *implementing* my strategies in the most advantageous way?"

In the words of wisdom attributed to Confucius, "Person who runs off in four directions at once, have hard time getting act together."

The key to scheduling your time is to focus on *objectives,* not on *activities.* You tell me you work *hard*, I ask you *on what do you work hard?*

I would suggest that you keep a master schedule that will outline how you will spend every week of your life during the next year implementing the strategies you have developed. Next, keep a weekly schedule showing how you will spend every day of that week implementing your strategies. Then keep a daily schedule showing how you will spend every *minute* of that day working toward your objectives.

Set deadlines for every task you set for yourself! Constantly practice doing everything better, in *less* time!

Remember, for the professional salesperson, every minute that you spend doing something other than working toward your objectives is a minute lost.

STEP #5—You guessed it: Work Your Schedule!

The best-planned schedule won't work *unless you do!*

If you have carefully scheduled your time, and built in enough flexibilities to allow for delays and unexpected opportunities, it is almost always better to *follow* that schedule.

The big question to ask before you tear off on a tangent is not "What will it *do* for me?" but "What will it do to move me toward my objectives?"

STEP #6—Evaluate, adjust, and improve!

You are not in a popularity contest with yourself, you are a professional salesperson who is constantly checking to see if you hit your targets!

The basis of every evaluation ought to be, "Did this action move me toward my objectives? Was it effective? Was it as effective as it could have been?"

As you answer those questions, make adjustments by asking even harder questions. "How could I have done it better? How could I have done it in less *time,* without loss of effectivensss? What improvements do I need to make? Am I taking advantage of *all* of the resources available to me?"

WHAT HAPPENS WHEN YOU MOBILIZE?

Have you ever seen a salesperson who starts out everyday with the primary objective of making a sale? That may be a good approach for the beginner because, after all, making sales is what this business is all about.

But that outlook has some problem areas. Let's take a look at some scenarios to see what often happens:

SCENARIO #1:

The salesperson hits the ground running and the first call results in a sale. From there it can go in one of two directions. Hopefully, the early success will inspire the salesperson to try to make as many sales as possible for that day.

However, most people who are living for their next sale tend to go the opposite route. They tend to quit for the day. The early success often is seen as a cause for celebration. The person might say, "I've already made more money today than I made all last week, so I'll take off the rest of the day and play golf."

SCENARIO #2:

The salesperson hits the ground running, works hard all morning, but is unable to make a sale. The person who lives for the next sale tends to get discouraged and to have self-doubts. Thus, it becomes easier to stretch out that lunch break. And, it becomes harder to maintain enthusiasm after several unsuccessful calls.

SCENARIO #3:

The salesperson starts out like a house afire and makes many sales over a period of several weeks. After weeks of running around all day, every day, putting in endless hours, the person gets burned out and might say, "It's just not worth it!" Many potentially great salespeople have left the field before their careers ever really got off the ground because they burned out very early in the game.

Mobilization Helps You Take The Long View

Professional salespeople who take the long view are able to pace themselves because they concentrate on building a sales career. They are able to maintain their enthusiasm because they manage their work by goals and objectives.

The most successful people in sales, year after year, are those who have established and are constantly working toward long-range goals and objectives. They are able to be more productive because they can schedule their work for maximum advantage. If they meet with discouragement early in the day, they remind themselves that the law of averages works in their favor. They know that if they continue to contact enough people, they will get enough presentations, and if they make enough good strong presentations, they will make enough sales to meet the goals they have set for themselves.

This professional attitude opens several doors toward greater success.

First, it enables the person to be more objective in self-evaluation and identifying areas of needed improvement. The person who is motivated by career goals can critique a presentation and close attempt that failed, with a view toward improving and refining his or her skills.

Secondly, it enables you to concentrate on what will build up the most repeat business. When each sale is seen as unconnected with previous sales, the tendency is to feel as if you are starting over on every call. A more systematic approach enables you to increase your sales vertically; to build your sales volume by selling more to fewer customers. The results are that you make more money with less effort.

Thirdly, the sales career professional is less likely to put undue pressure on individual prospects. The amateur who lives from one sale to the next often offends the prospective customer by excessive aggressiveness. The "Johnny-one-sale" may even beg for an order because he needs the sale so badly. Pressure tactics and begging for orders are demeaning, both to the customer and the salesperson, and tend to close the door to future sales.

If you want to make a success out of a sales career, don't just get yourself hyped up with enthusiasm. Concentrate on mobilizing all your resources in a steady, systematic process of building your territory into a goldmine. You'll be happier, more productive, and more stable.

* * *

BECOME A TERRITORIAL GOAL-SETTER

1. What would I like my territory to be like five years from now? _____
_____
_____

2. Are my ambitions for my territory realistic? ___
_____
_____

3. What would be the benefits to me from reaching this goal? _____
_____
_____

MANAGE YOUR TERRITORY BY OBJECTIVES

List three major things you will have to do to make your goals become reality.

1. _____
2. _____
3. _____

PLAN YOUR STRATEGIES

Study your list of accounts to determine how much volume each account produces and how much time you spend with each account. Are you spending most of your time on the accounts that produce most of your sales volume?

YES ( )   NO ( )

Plan strategies to adjust your time/volume ratios:

1. _____
2. _____
3. _____

NOTE: The key to managing your territory is to plan every move so that it contributes to the objectives that will take you to your goals.

SCHEDULE YOUR WORK

The key to scheduling your time is to focus on objectives—not on activities.

DO YOU:

1. Keep a master schedule outlining your work schedule for a year?

        YES ( )   NO ( )

1. Keep a weekly schedule showing how you will spend each day?

        YES ( )   NO ( )

3. Keep a daily schedule showing how you will spend each hour?

        YES ( )   NO ( )

4. Set deadlines for each task you have outlined?

        YES ( )   NO ( )

WORK YOUR SCHEDULE

The best-planned schedule won't work unless you do! The big question to ask before tearing off on a tangent is, "What will it do to move me toward my objectives?" Do you strive to spend your days carefully following your planned schedule?

Always ( )   Often ( )   Seldom ( )

EVALUATE, ADJUST, AND IMPROVE

As a professional salesperson, you will want to keep checking on every action to see if you hit your targets. This list of questions is designed to give you a guide for those check-ups:

1. Did this action move me toward my goals?
2. Was it effective?
3. Was it as effective as it could have been?
4. How could I have done it better?
5. How could I have done it in less time, without loss of effectiveness?
6. Am I taking advantage of all the resources available to me?

6.

Boost Your Selling Brainpower

"What's the difference between the SONY and the RCA television sets?" I asked the department store salesman.

"A hundred and fifteen dollars!" he said.

Can you believe he actually thought I was so ignorant that I could not read the price tags?

What I wanted was for him to tell me something that would justify the higher cost of the TV I wanted to buy; *and he blew it!*

There's an old saying that goes, "What you don't know, can't hurt you." When it comes to selling, don't *believe* that. What you don't know about *selling*, about your *company*, about your *products* and *services*, and what you don't know about your *industry* can cost you plenty.

But there's a positive side to that: What you *do know* can *help* you sell! Brainpower, properly directed, becomes selling power.

Whoever said that knowledge is power must have had selling in mind. The professional salesperson knows that many, many sales have been made because of what the salesperson knows; and that the professional salesperson knows that many, many sales have been lost because of what a salesperson did *not* know.

That is why the professional seeks to learn everything possible and to become the company field expert out in the territory.

Did you notice that I said "tries to become" an expert; not "acts like an expert." There is absolutely no place in professionalism for the "know it all" attitude. The true professional is wise enough to *use* knowledge—not to flaunt it!

The fact that you are reading this book is a strong indication that you want to increase your knowledge—your selling brainpower. You don't need to be sold on learning, so I'm going to be very specific about what you need to know to increase your selling ability, and about how to develop that knowledge.

FIVE AREAS WHERE KNOWLEDGE IS POWER

What do you need to know to become a powerful professional salesperson? There are at least five areas in which knowledge is selling power.

AREA #1: You need to know how to sell! That is so obvious that most of us tend to overlook it.

Alexander Pope said, "A little learning is a dang'rous thing," and some salespeople have just enough learning to make them dangerous.

A minister, speaking just before me to a group of sales managers in Milwaukee, told the Bible story about how Samson killed a thousand Phillistines with the jawbone of an ass. *"That's* no big deal," said one of the sales managers. "I've got a salesman who kills at least that many sales each month with the same weapon—the jawbone of an ass!"

Knowledge of how to sell is a little like water. When it is shallow, it rambles all over the place, and creates a swamp, a bog, a slushy mess that nobody can get through. You've seen sales presentations like that, haven't you? I certainly have seen plenty during my years of training and travelling with the sales forces of my client companies. I've seen many salespeople who know a little bit about everything, but not much about selling.

But sales knowledge that is concentrated, and deep, is like a river. It creates movement, it creates power, it creates force, and vitality. Like the river, when that knowledge is dammed up by an obstruction, it concentrates its energy and breaks through.

Think about your sales presentation the next time you watch Olympic ice skaters perform on television. They perform the most difficult movements with style and grace! Their movements are elegance in motion. When they make a mistake, or their routine is interrupted, they pick right back up and keep going! That kind of excellence comes only from practice, practice, and *more* practice. They have drilled and drilled until they have so mastered the fundamentals that they don't even have to *think* about them. Thus, when the spotlight is on them, they are free to concentrate on expression, on timing, and on communicating with their audience.

Whatever else you seek to learn, learn how to make your presentation with *power,* with *force,* and with *vitality.* The only way to do that is to practice, practice, practice. And, when you've made that presentation a thousand times, *practice* some more!

AREA #2: Know your company! The salesperson is the only person from a company that many people ever see. When you are in the presence of a customer, you become the company to that customer!

I once walked into a furniture store in the northeast where I was doing marketing research for a successful retail chain. I looked around until the salesperson came over and made the presentation, and I said, "That's nice . . . I like the way it looks. . . . But your company; I've never heard of you. . . . Are you new?" I looked at him, and listened to hear what he would say.

"Oh, no!" he said. "We've been selling furniture for more than 20 years. . . . We've got more than 20 stores throughout the United States. We've got lots of happy customers."

That salesperson knew enough about the company to build my confidence in that company's reliability. Later, I told the president of that company about this young man, and he was promoted to a higher-paying position.

Why do you think major corporations spend millions and millions of dollars on advertising brand names? They are willing to spend all that money because they know that people buy from companies they have come to know and trust.

The more you *know* about your company, the more you can give *facts* about that company that will inspire confidence in new prospects, and keep your regular customers *loyal*.

AREA #3: Where knowledge is selling power—know your products and the services your company offers!

When a customer asks, "Does it come in red?" or, "Why did they put the handle on that side?" or, "How much floor space will it take up?" or, "How soon can you ship it?" that customer wants information, not a bunch of sales puff.

One of the most common complaints consumers and professional buyers make is that they can't get a straight answer to a simple question about the product (when they ask a salesperson). And, do you know why they can't get a straight answer? Research shows that the most common reason salespeople refuse to give a straight answer is that they don't *know* enough about the product or service.

You *owe* it to your busy customer to know everything you need to know about your products and services to answer quickly and concisely at least 99% of the questions that customers might ask.

A salesperson couldn't believe it when he walked into a customer's office one day and saw that *his* machine had been replaced by a competitor's inferior product. "Why did you buy *that*?" he asked the customer. "Because that *new* machine has *two* memory banks on it, and we need two memory banks."

Do you know what that salesperson *did?* He said, *"Oh!"* and walked out!

"You *Dummy!*" his sales manager shouted when told about the loss of a big office machine supply customer. "The machine you sold him two years ago does have two memory banks on it!"

"I didn't know *that!*" said our hero. The salesman had lost a valuable customer because of what he didn't know about the product he was selling.

What you know about your complete product line, and all of the services your company offers, is one of the best measures of how professional you are as a salesperson. Professionals are inquisitive, they are insatiable questioners, they are always open to learn because they know that product or service knowledge is like money in the bank.

But here's an important point: *If you don't know, don't fake it!* You'll gain much more respect by saying simply, "I don't know—*but* I'll *find out* and let you know *right* away!"

AREA #4: Know your industry!

Who buys the products or services your company sells and why do they buy them? How do your products contribute to the lives and businesses of the customers who buy them? How are your services and products used? What trends have affected your industry in recent years, and what trends are emerging that could affect your customers in the future? These, and many more questions, can provide information that can help you sell.

An important part of this area of knowledge is information about your competitors. Who are they? What do they sell? How are their products inferior to yours? How are their products superior to yours? How do they sell? *Whom* do they sell? What do they *tell* your customers? What *gaps* are there in their product lines?

Believe me, some of your competitors are highly trained professionals, and they know more about you than you can imagine. Professional salespeople don't lie awake at nights worrying about what's happening in their industries and what their competitors are up to; they just keep an ear to the ground, and they observe everything that goes on around them!

How do you keep up? Read trade journals, ask questions of your customers and people within your company, study ads and sales literature from all of the companies that serve your industry, stay alert, and observe everything that goes on around you.

Some of the best advice any salesperson can heed is, "Shut up, and listen!" The more knowledgeable you are about your industry, the more likely your customers are to respect you as your company's field expert.

AREA #5: Know your customers!

Frank Bettger was one of the best salesmen who ever lived. He wrote a book titled, *How I Raised Myself From Failure To Success In Selling,* which Dale Carnegie called "the most helpful and inspiring book on salesmanship that I have ever read." In fact, when I was president of the National Speakers Association, we offered the work as a classic to all our members.

"The one biggest secret of selling *anything*," said Frank Bettger, "is: Try to find out what people want, and then help them get it."

What a powerful insight! "Try to find out what people want, and then help them get it!"

Mr. Bettger goes on to tell how an educator, named Louis Holden, got the first donation Andrew Carnegie *ever* made to a school. In exactly four minutes, Dr. Holden collected *$100,000* from a man who opened the interview by saying, "I don't believe in giving money to colleges." How did he turn it around? He appealed to Mr. Carnegie's desire to help young people get started in life.

"Young man," said Carnegie, laughing as he handed over the check, "if you ever come to see me *again*, don't stay so long. Your call just cost me *$25,000* a minute."

But it cost him a lot more than that because, during his life, Andrew Carnegie gave more than $100,000,000 for the advancement of education.

Mr. Bettger concludes, "When you show a man what he wants, he'll move heaven and earth to get it."

Let me ask you a simple question: How can you *show* a person how to *get* what he wants, if you don't *know* what he wants?

Professional salespeople become consultants to their customers. They know more about their customer's needs, in their area of expertise, than the customer knows! They study the customer, they draw him out with questions, they observe *everything* that customer does, and listen to everything that customer *says*.

So, there you have them—five areas where knowledge is selling power. I feel so strongly about them I wish I could make them five commandments of selling brainpower. They would read like this:

1. Thou shalt know *how to sell!*
2. Thou shalt know *thy company!*
3. Thou shalt know *thy company's products and services!*
4. Thou shalt know *thy industry!*
5. Thou shalt know *thy customer!*

But I can't make commandments. I can only promise you this: If you will adopt them as your priorities for learning, you can become your company's field expert in your territory; you can join the major leagues as a professional salesperson!

What you know can help you sell; because brainpower, properly directed, becomes selling power!

* * *

RATE YOUR SALES KNOWLEDGE

To help you determine your selling brainpower, we are going to give you a series of statements about each of the five areas in which a salesperson needs specialized knowledge. Rate yourself on a scale of 1-10 and set a goal for improving your knowledge in each area.

HOW TO SELL

I am familiar with all phases of selling. I can give a sales presentation with self-confidence, ease, and power. I have practiced so much that every word, every movement flows smoothly toward a natural close.

MY RATING: (1 2 3 4 5 6 7 8 9 10)

MY GOAL FOR IMPROVEMENT: _____

KNOWLEDGE OF MY COMPANY

I know enough about my company to easily build confidence in all my prospects. I am familiar with its history, its methods of doing business, its policies, and its strong selling points to persuade my prospects it is to their advantage to buy from us.

MY RATING: (1 2 3 4 5 6 7 8 9 10)

MY GOAL FOR IMPROVEMENT: _____

KNOWLEDGE OF PRODUCTS & SERVICES

I am completely familiar with all of the products and/or services my company offers my customers. I pride myself on being able to answer any question about the things I sell, with complete confidence and accuracy. I can give a thorough and convincing presentation on anything my company sells.

MY RATING: (1 2 3 4 5 6 7 8 9 10)

MY GOAL FOR IMPROVEMENT: _____

KNOWLEDGE OF INDUSTRY

I know who buys the kinds of products and/or services my company sells and why they buy them. I am familiar with all of the practices, trends, and important factors that affect my industry. I know my competitors and what they are up to. I know how to sell against them.

MY RATING: (1 2 3 4 5 6 7 8 9 10)

MY GOAL FOR IMPROVEMENT: _____

KNOWLEDGE OF MY CUSTOMERS

I am familiar enough with all my customers and prospects that I understand exactly what they want, and how they can get it through what I have to offer. I make it a regular practice to study my customers, to ask questions that give me information I need to know in servicing them, and I observe everything that will give me insight into that customer's needs.

MY RATING: (1 2 3 4 5 6 7 8 9 10)

MY GOAL FOR IMPROVEMENT: _____

7.

Turn What You Know Into What You Can Spend

If brainpower is selling power, why aren't all geniuses rich?

It's a valid question that deserves a straight answer. Many very knowledgeable salespeople are failures because they don't have the wisdom to use what they know to close sales.

Said positively, what you know is important, but how you use that knowledge is even more important. *Knowledge* is a store of information, but *wisdom* is the productive use of that information.

How do you turn knowledge into sales?

Think for a minute about the big powerful engine in an automobile. It's just a heavy hunk of metal until you turn on the ignition and hit the starter. But, it's still good for nothing except to drink gas and make noise until you put the transmission in gear. Then that engine will carry you across the United States.

Do you know why they call it a transmission? Because it takes all of that power the engine generates and transmits it to the wheels where it becomes useful.

The amateur salesperson cranks up that engine of knowledge and makes a lot of noise, consumes a lot of energy, blows off a lot of smoke, and pollutes the customer's home or office. But the professional salesperson quietly cranks up the knowledge engine, slips the transmission of wisdom into gear, and gently moves toward making the sale.

But remember this: The more efficient the engine, the better performance it gives, and the less energy it consumes. Don't forget to keep the engine of knowledge in good working order and finely tuned.

There are five tested and proven steps to turning knowledge power into sales power: five ways to turn what you know into what you can spend.

STEP #1: Use knowledge to spot problems, needs, and opportunities.

That sounds simple, doesn't it? But don't let its simplicity fool you. Even the most successful salespeople often overlook potential sales, because they fail to understand the problem, or need, their customer has.

For example, International Business Machines was in the business of making office machines a few decades ago—but so were many other companies. At some point, some person on the staff discovered that what their potential customers needed was not office machines, but better ways to process data. IBM soon became synonymous with data processing.

Again, in about 1950, someone at IBM realized that what their customers needed was not to simply process data, but to gather, analyze, and utilize information. So they developed a sophisticated line of computers and began to sell "management information systems."

IBM's customers were not in the market for business machines, they wanted to be able to process data, and manipulate information—and there's a big difference.

Sometimes it takes a lot of knowledge, and wisdom, to spot the customer's real problem. Even the customer might not be aware of what the problem is. The smart salesperson seeks first to discover the real need—both as it really is and as the customer perceives it to be—and only then seeks to fill that need.

For example, a new car salesperson might be told by a prospect, "I want a car that gets good mileage, is cheap to operate, and has a good trade-in value." Now, that sounds pretty simple, and pretty precise, doesn't it?

However, as the prospect talks further, it becomes clear that the stated need is not the real need at all. During the interview, the customer asks about custom interiors, a stereo system, air conditioning, deluxe hubcaps, and vinyl tops. The alert salesperson picks up the fact that the prospect's real needs run along the lines of comfort, prestige, and driving pleasure.

One of the best ways to fully understand this principle is to study the highly effective television commercials put together by real professionals. McDonald's doesn't sell hamburgers, they sell the customer a "break today!" Ma Bell doesn't sell long distance calls, they sell an opportunity to "reach out and touch someone!" Toyota doesn't sell cars, they sell a "feeling!" And, Kodak long ago discovered that people don't want to take pictures, they want to *capture memories!* But more than that, they learned that people get upset when the memories they thought they had captured, don't come back. So now they tell you to "trust those special moments to Kodak film." Whom are they kidding? They make film, but they sell memories and trust, which is what people want to buy.

"What do *you* sell?" I often ask salespeople. The order-taker and the peddler tell the names of their products. But the real professionals smile and ask me what do I want to buy.

The number one way to turn knowledge power into selling power is to use it to spot problems. Find a need and fill it; find a desire and satisfy it; find an opportunity for your customer and take home a signed order.

How do you do that? That is such an important question that I will devote an entire chapter to it later. For now let me give you a simple two-word answer—*ask questions!* Your knowledge can help you to know the right questions to ask to spot the *real* problem.

When you become a master problem-spotter, you can turn knowledge into *sales!*

STEP #2: Show the customer how what you are selling will solve the problem, or meet the need.

People will cheerfully pay dearly for solutions to their problems.

Why do people gladly pay higher prices for one or two items at a curb store? They don't call them "convenience" stores for nothing! Nobody wants to sweat a long line in a supermarket for a deodorant stick! Convenience stores sell *convenience!*

It's not enough to say, "Yessir, I think this service will solve your problem!" You must show that customer exactly how it will solve his problem.

Salespeople tend to think about features of their products. They talk about the laminated plastic tabletop, or the handle on top of a widget. But the customer says, "So what?" What the customer wants to know is that the table is easy to keep clean and will resist scratches, heat, and household chemicals. That customer needs to know that the handle on the top makes the widget easy to carry!

Put yourself into the customer's position. "What's in it for me?" That's what the customer wants to know. Show your customers what's in it for them! Show your customers exactly how a feature will benefit them!

Let me do exactly what I'm telling you to do by an example from Frank Bettger's book, *How I Raised Myself From Failure To Success In Selling*. A successful businessman named Scott had told Mr. Bettger he was 63 years old and quit buying insurance long ago! His children were all grown, his wife was well fixed with paid-up insurance, and his company supplied adequate coverage in the event of his death. Now most insurance salespeople would have thanked the man for his time and walked away empty-handed. *Not Frank Bettger!* Listen to the conversation that followed.

Bettger said, "Mr. Scott, a man who has been as successful as you have surely must have some interests outside of your family and your business, perhaps a hospital, religious work, missionary or charitable work. . . . Did you ever consider that when you die your support will be withdrawn? Wouldn't this loss seriously handicap or even mean the discontinuance of some splendid work?"

Mr. Scott told him about three missionaries in Nicaragua he supported. Through asking questions, Bettger learned that one of those missionary teams consisted of Mr. Scott's *son* and daughter-in-law, and that he was planning to visit their work site soon.

Frank Bettger said, "Mr. Scott, when you go down to Nicaragua, wouldn't you be very happy to tell your son and his little family that you have just completed arrangements and, if anything ever happens to you, a *check* will come to them *every month,* so their work may continue? And wouldn't you like to write a letter to the other two missionaries, giving them the same message?"

He walked out of that office that day with a check for nearly $9,000—and that was when $9,000 was a lot of money.

He had used his knowledge of his product, and the knowledge he gained through asking questions, to show the customer exactly how his product would solve that customer's problem.

STEP #3: Help your customer implement the solution!

Make it easy and convenient for the customer to buy and use your product or service.

Amateur salespeople always distort the golden rule to read: "Do unto others and *split!*" Get the order and get out of there! Professionals follow through to make sure that the customer is as happy after the sale as when he or she signed the order.

Make sure that the product or service does all that you have promised that it will. Show the customer additional, or side benefits that were not even expected. Help the customer feed the product into his or her system. If it's something to be re-sold by the customer, help with display, advertising, and training his or her salespeople how to sell it to their customers.

Professional salespeople try every way possible to make a customer happy because they know that customer is their best prospect for future sales.

Turn What You Know Into What You Can Spend 83

STEP #4: Track the results!

If the solution you have offered doesn't work, find out why and come up with a way to make it work for your customer.

The customer who says, "The only time I see you is when you want an order," is not likely to be a customer for very long. If some mix-up in shipping results in the order being delivered incorrectly, assume the responsibility for getting it straightened out. It matters little whose fault it was, but it matters much who gets it straightened out.

When the customer sees that you are genuinely interested in his or her well-being, you are well on your way to becoming a trusted friend. You become a respected professional and the customer becomes a client.

Finally, for turning knowledge into sales, is . . .

STEP #5: Use the information you gain through tracking results to find more solutions!

Why do you think big companies spend millions to get celebrities to endorse their products? It's simple . . . it works!

An old pro in the furniture business was asked to explain to his fellow salesmen how he had sold five boxcar loads of furniture in one week.

"You see this newspaper ad?" he asked as he held it up. "A retailer in my territory told me he had sold a boxcar load of our furniture with that ad the weekend before. I asked him if I could have a copy and told him I wouldn't show it to anybody in his town. He was glad to give it to me because I'd brought him a lot of ads.

"Well, I took that ad to five of my *other* dealers and told them how it had sold for the first guy. . . . Every one of them ordered a boxcar load of furniture!

"And, you know something," he added, "every one of those dealers had met me at the door and told me business was lousy . . . that they didn't even want to talk to me!"

That fellow had quit taking orders for furniture and had started selling results! And, because he's a professional, he'll remember that ad promotion next year!

A professional saleswoman I know used a single testimonial letter from a happy customer to gain 65 more happy customers for her cosmetics company.

"I never have any trouble getting in to see my customers," said an industrial salesman. "They look on me as a business partner because I care as much about their business as they do." And then he added something very important, *"When they have a problem, they call me!"*

You go to a lot of trouble and expense to sell a customer. Make sure you sell that customer all that you can, and get that customer to help you sell other customers.

Peddlers make cold calls; *professionals* build and build onto relationships with happy customers.

IT'S NOT WHAT YOU KNOW, BUT HOW YOU USE IT

So, why aren't all geniuses rich? They haven't learned how to turn what they know into what they can *spend*.

What you know is important, but how you use what you know is even more important. Use what you know to spot problems, to show your customers solutions, to help your customers implement the solutions, to track the results, and use the information you gain from tracking the results to find *more* solutions.

Become your company's field expert in your territory, and turn knowledge into sales!

* * *

APPLICATION EXERCISE

We gave you five steps to turning knowledge into sales. As you review each of the five steps, think of a customer you have sold by using the step effectively. Analyze how you used that step to make a sale. And, plan a strategy for using it with at least one other customer.

1. USE KNOWLEDGE TO SPOT PROBLEMS, NEEDS, AND OPPORTUNITIES:

   MY CUSTOMER: _____
   MY ANALYSIS: _____
   _____

   STRATEGY FOR OTHER CUSTOMERS: ____
   _____
   _____

2. USE KNOWLEDGE TO SHOW PROSPECT HOW YOUR PRODUCT WILL MEET THE NEED:

   MY CUSTOMER: _____
   MY ANALYSIS: _____
   _____

   STRATEGY FOR OTHER CUSTOMERS: ____
   _____
   _____

3. HELP YOUR CUSTOMER TO IMPLEMENT THE SOLUTION:

   MY CUSTOMER: _____

MY ANALYSIS: _____

STRATEGY FOR OTHER CUSTOMERS: ____

4. USE KNOWLEDGE TO TRACK THE RESULTS OF THE SOLUTION THE CUSTOMER HAS IMPLEMENTED:

MY CUSTOMER: _____
MY ANALYSIS: _____

STRATEGY FOR OTHER CUSTOMERS: ____

5. USE INFORMATION FROM TRACKING TO FIND MORE SOLUTIONS AND SALES:

MY CUSTOMER: _____
MY ANALYSIS: _____

STRATEGY FOR OTHER CUSTOMERS: ____

EXERCISE FOR FURTHER GROWTH

List below three customers you have not been able to sell. Plan how you will use each of the steps outlined above to sell each of those customers:

1. _____
2. _____
3. _____

8.

Build Your Communication Skills; Boost Your Personal Selling Power

The single most important way to boost your personal selling power, and increase your income, is to become more effective in communicating!

At the outbreak of World War II, masses of people throughout Europe were caught in the hopelessness of despair. The sophisticated war machine of Nazi Germany, and the fanatic fervor of Adolph Hitler threatened to crush everything the people held dear.

Then one voice began to ring out a message of courage and hope of victory. It was the voice of Sir Winston Churchill, prime minister of Great Britain. "Victory at all costs," he cried out in his raspy, almost whining voice, "Victory however long and hard the road may be, for without victory there is no survival."

Through the static and interference, the primitive radios picked up that challenge and carried it to millions of frightened Europeans. They arose in response and defended their homelands with a spirit that made it their "finest hour."

Winston Churchill was a man of courage, a man of principle, a man of hope; but he was also a *skilled communicator.* He was able to motivate people to do things through effective communication.

Whether you are trying to sell hope and courage to an endangered world, or merely attempting to sell a widget to a little old school teacher, the principles of effective communication are the same.

In fact, effective selling is effective communication!

I once heard a potential customer pay the saddest compliment that can be paid to a salesperson. This potential customer said, "I hated to see him lose his job because he was one of the nicest people who ever called on me. Of course, I never bought anything from him, but I always liked him." On checking further, I found that the salesperson was that way with everyone in his territory, which is the reason he lost his job. Everybody liked him, but nobody bought anything from him.

In selling, it is not enough to simply communicate; you must communicate *effectively*. It is never enough to have personal power; you must have personal selling power if you would be a successful salesperson.

Effective communication is a two-way exchange of information that produces a desired response. What a perfect definition of selling! You exchange information with a client in a way that motivates the client to buy.

THREE SKILLS OF EFFECTIVE COMMUNICATION

There are basically three skills you need for effective communication. I want to give you a little formula by which you can remember them. It is the *S.L.O.* method of communicating. *S* stands for speaking, or sending messages; *L* stands for listening; and *O* stands for observing. Speaking, listening, and observing—the three skills of effective communication. Let's look at all three in depth.

Speaking

You send messages to your prospective client in a variety of ways. Speaking is the most obvious way, but everything about you and everything you do sends messages.

Now that is so obvious that most of us tend to take it for granted. To help you avoid that, I want to use a couple of ridiculous illustrations.

If you were to walk in to see a prospect tomorrow—a prospect you had never seen—and before you said a word, you pulled out a big pistol and placed it on the table between you, what kind of message would that send?

Or what kind of message would you send if you walked into a plush office, dressed in a bathing suit, and began pulling product samples out of a beach bag?

In either case, you would be considered a nut to be gotten rid of as quickly and safely as possible, or a clown who was there to waste the prospect's time.

Your appearance, your personal mannerisms, and your facial expressions all send messages to your prospects. Yet many people who are out there beating their brains out day after day trying to sell, pay almost no attention to these important message senders.

As a professional salesperson, one of the most important steps in effective communication is to present yourself to your prospect in the *proper* light. Give careful personal attention to *everything* about you, and everything you do, to make sure that your customers see you in the way you want them to see you.

If you present yourself as warm and approachable, as competent and capable, as sincere and trustworthy, and genuinely interested in your customer, you can open the door to talk business. After all, isn't that what you are there for?

And, did you notice that I said that one of the three skills of effective communication is speaking? Did I say *talking?* No, I said *speaking!* There is a big difference! Professional salespeople know that they are not in the business of making social calls, they don't drop by a customer's home or place of business just to chitchat. Of course they're sociable, they're friendly, and they're always pleasant.

But people expect to be sold. They expect the salesperson to sell them on his or her product or service, and to assure them of the reliability of the company he or she represents.

I talked with an old pro who represents one of the largest heavyweight equipment manufacturers in the United States. He is so well-liked by the people in his territory, that when he was recently named "Salesman of the Year" by his company, his customers got together and gave him an appreciation dinner.

When I asked him the secret of his success, he said, "I have never been in a customer's office without my bag! When I walk in the door, they know I'm there to do business!"

The professional salesperson opens the door to talk business and then keeps the interview on track. Ever so gently, the effective communicator constantly brings the topic of conversation back to the *main* theme of the presentation.

What we're really talking about is *targeted* communication! Some people use the "sawed-off shotgun" approach to communicating. They walk in talking about everything from weather to politics, to sports, and talk as rapidly as they can for as long as the prospect will listen. When they finish, everybody—especially the prospect—is confused about who they are and what they are selling. All they know for sure is that the salesperson is a big talker, and that he or she is excited about *something.*

Professional salespeople use a *targeted* communication approach. They know they will only have one good shot, so they organize what they will say, plan what they will present, practice the way they will say it, and zero-in on their target. And, what is the target of all sales representatives? The bullseye for every sales presentation is closing the sale! Those who become successful salespeople learn to *target everything* they *say* and *do* toward *one* goal—*getting the order!*

Does this mean that the professional salesperson runs roughshod over the feelings of the prospect? *No!* A thousand times, *No!* I'm going to tell you how to avoid that by using the other two important elements of the formula for effective communication.

But for now, I want you to understand this: If you want to build your sales communication skills, learn to speak effectively, learn to organize what you will say and say what you have organized, learn to use strong selling words. Learn to use action words. Get excited, get enthusiastic, get motivated to motivate your prospects.

Remember this: As a professional salesperson, you are a professional speaker. To boost your selling power, study the best professional speakers you know, and cultivate good speaking skills.

Listening

Part two of the Qubein principle of effective communication is listening! Did you notice I did not say *hearing?* You hear the noise of traffic, you hear the background music in an elevator, you hear the jet as it goes over your head.

But, if you are a professional salesperson, and an effective communicator, you *listen* to your prospect. Hearing is the physical response of your ears to sound stimulation, but *listening* is the combined action of your ears and your mind to pay attention to what your prospect is saying.

If you listen, if you pay attention, you *invest* yourself in the expressions of the needs and the interests of your prospect. Some of the most clever television commercials in recent years are in the series done by E.F. Hutton. You've seen them, I'm sure. They open up with a busy scene in which a lot of people are doing many things, but, when E.F. Hutton talks, *everything* stops—and people listen! The idea is that people who want to make money from their investments listen to what E.F. Hutton has to say.

That suggests an image that every person who wants to become a professional salesperson must remember: When the *prospect* speaks, the professional salesperson listens! If you want to make money in investments, the commercials say, stop everything and listen when E.F. Hutton speaks. If you want to make money in sales, stop everything and *listen* when your prospect speaks.

Why is active listening so important in effective communication?

First, it shows that you are *genuinely interested* in your prospect! You can only pay attention, you can only invest yourself, in a person in whom you are interested. When the prospect sees that you are sincerely interested in what *he or she* has to say, that prospect will respond with interest to what *you* have to say. Listen to the prospect if you would have the prospect listen to you.

Secondly, when you listen, you *learn!* You learn valuable information that can help you close the sale. You learn what the prospect *needs,* what the prospect *wants,* what the prospect *doesn't* want. Through listening, you learn what excites your prospect. Someone has called it finding your client's "hot button."

Thirdly, by listening to your prospect, you *discover.* You discover false impressions the prospect may have about you, or your company, or your product—false impressions you can correct! Through listening, the effective communicator often discovers that the customer needs *10 items,* instead of *the one* the salesperson is trying to sell. By listening, you discover problems that make what you are selling absolutely essential to your prospect.

Finally, when you listen, you involve your prospect in the selling process! If the first words you expect to hear your prospect say are *"Yes, I'll buy,"* you will more likely hear that prospect say *"No, I won't buy!"* The involved prospect, becomes an interested prospect. And, do you know what the professional salesperson calls an interested prospect? *A customer!* And the best way to involve your prospect is to listen!

If you would become an effective selling communicator, learn to speak—not just talk! If you would become an effective selling communicator, learn to listen—not just to hear!

Observing

The third part of the *S.L.O.* formula for effective communication is observe!

Did you notice that I did not say learn to *see?* Seeing is the natural response of your eyes to visual images. I said learn to *observe!* And what is observing? It is paying attention, investing your interest in the signals that your prospect is sending.

The effective selling communicator learns to look for the buying signals that indicate it is time to start the close, to observe the signs of confusion that say, "Tell me more," to watch the facial expressions that indicate distraction or disinterest, to sense the changes of mood that indicate it's time to move into a new phase of the presentation.

When my car was not running right, I took it to a highly professional auto mechanic. He connected the engine to a diagnostic machine with a very complex system of wires. That machine showed instantly what was going on in every part of that engine. *"Aha!"* the mechanic said triumphantly, "there's your trouble! I can fix it in no time!"

The professional salesperson learns to use observation as a tool for monitoring all of the signals the prospect is sending. When something is *wrong,* the effective communicator can fix it in no time. When a signal says something is going *right,* that salesperson can build on it to move toward the target—closing the sale!

Build Your Communication Skills; Boost Your Selling Power

The single most important way to boost your selling power, and your income, is to become more effective in communicating! You can do that by sharpening your skills of *speaking, listening,* and *observing.*

These are your specialized skills that enable you to render a unique service to your clients and make you a professional salesperson!

* * *

GETTING A HANDLE
ON THE S.L.O. PRINCIPLE

Define each of the six words below, based on what you learned from this chapter:

1. Talking: _____

2. Speaking: _____

3. Hearing: _____

4. Listening: _____

5. Seeing: _____

6. Observing: _____

NONVERBAL COMMUNICATION

Everything about you communicates something to your prospect. Below are some desirable traits your customer is looking for. Beside each, list some ways you seek to convey the trait by your appearance and mannerisms:

1. Approachability: _____
_____

2. Competence: _____
_____

3. Businesslike manner: _____
_____

4. Trustworthiness: _____
_____

5. Sincere interest: _____
_____

TRUE OR FALSE?

To help you review the S.L.O. method of communicating, check each of the following statements as true or false.

	TRUE	FALSE
1. Chatting about the weather, sports or politics helps make sales.	___	___
2. Making social calls is a good investment of time.	___	___
3. People expect to be sold.	___	___
4. The professional salesperson constantly brings the topic of conversation back to the main theme of the presentation.	___	___
5. When you listen, you invest yourself in your client.	___	___
6. By listening, you involve your prospect, and an involved prospect is an interested prospect.	___	___
7. When a prospect begins a sentence that shows he/she has a false impression of your product, you must interrupt, and correct the prospect.	___	___
8. Your effectiveness as a communicator can be increased by observing your client's buying signals.	___	___
9. Facial expressions are of little value in determining when the client is distracted or disinterested.	___	___
10. "Tell me more" is an effective expression for getting the client to talk.	___	___

Answers: 1, 2, 7 and 9 are False; 3, 4, 5, 6, 8, and 10 are True.

EXERCISES FOR FURTHER GROWTH

1. To practice your speaking skills, pick three of the most important statements from your presentation and practice them until you can say them exactly as you would like the prospect to hear them.

2. To practice your listening skills, listen to three five-minute newscasts and write a summary of each story the newscaster gives. Pay particular attention to names, dates, and places.

3. To practice your observing skills, pick out a character in a TV show and make notes of every gesture the camera focuses on.

9.

Ten Ways To Add Power To Your Persuasion

The ultimate test of your selling effectiveness is your *power* to *persuade plenty* of *prospects* to *purchase* your *product* at a *profit*.

My favorite word in the English language is the word *persuade!* It describes, better than any other word, what I do all day long, every day! I love to persuade people to do positive things! If I didn't enjoy it, I would get out of the business of selling and teaching thousands of people each and every year how to sell and how to manage—in personal appearances and via my books, cassette albums, consulting services, and syndicated radio program.

Many of those people who hear me are very successful. My mother used to say to me, "Nido, if you would be successful, first you must walk hand-in-hand and side-by-side with successful people!" So, I observe successful salespeople everywhere I go. Do you know the *one thing* I have observed about *all* very successful salespeople? *They persuade with power!*

Does that mean that all successful salespeople have dynamic personalities? Does that mean they put a lot of pressure on their prospects? Does that mean they are aggressive, that they lack sensitivity? *No!* I am not talking about high pressure tactics, or out-talking a prospective buyer!

Some of the most successful salespeople I know are rather easy-going, some are even laid-back personality types. And *all* of them are very considerate of their prospective clients—they know that a prospect is their bread and butter, and their cake and ice cream. They are professionals who persuade their clients to buy. And, because they know that the best prospect for a future sale is a happy customer, they persuade again—they sell to sell again!

ADD POWER TO YOUR PERSUASION!

Do you want to boost your selling power? Then, add power to your persuasion! Let me give it to you in the form of a guarantee: If you learn enough from this chapter to increase your persuasive power by 10%, you can increase your sales by at least 10%!

How do you add power to your persuasion? How do you become more effective at persuading your customers to buy? Let's look at how the skilled professionals put power in their ability to persuade.

You might have guessed when I told you that my favorite word is persuade, that my favorite letter in the alphabet is the letter *"P,"* which is the first letter of persuade. That little letter *"P"* suggests *action*. It leads us to words like power, pow, pop, perform, and prod.

I want to give you 10 ways to add power to your persuasive ability. I call them the 10 "P's" of persuasion.

1. *Be Positive!* That's the first way to add power to your persuasion. One of the most successful insurance salesmen in

America is a country bumpkin from south Georgia, who says, "You can't no more sell something you *don't* believe in, than you can come back from some place you *ain't been!*"

Successful salespeople are *positive* people! They have a positive mental attitude about themselves, the companies they represent, the products or services they are selling, the prospects they are attempting to persuade, the country they live in—they are positive about everything!

Enthusiasm is contagious! The salesperson who is excited about life, and the work he or she is doing can persuade with power—because that salesperson can get other people excited.

2. *The second "P" of persuasion is Prospect!* Successful salespeople have learned to direct their persuasive power toward people who can buy and have good reasons to buy what they are selling.

One of the most obvious marks of an amateur at selling is that the person wastes days and days by attempting to persuade people who have no need or desire to buy, or people who have no authority to buy.

Professional salespeople concentrate on people who can buy, and people who have good reasons to buy what they are selling. You won't find them spilling their story to a secretary who won't let them in to see the decision-maker. When the secretary says, "Tell me what you are selling and I'll tell Mrs. Jones. . . . If she's interested, she'll call you . . .," the skilled persuader directs all efforts toward getting an appointment with the person who has the authority to buy.

In short, the powerful persuader targets all efforts at the person who has the resources, the possible motivation, and the authority to buy.

3. *The third "P" of powerful persuasion is Prepare.* Red Motley, who started *Parade Magazine,* once observed that the average American salesperson will work himself or herself to death trying to get an appointment. Finally, after working like crazy to get an appointment, they find themselves standing face to face with the *very* client or customer they've always hoped to be in front of—then they screw up the presentation!

They work so hard *getting* the appointment, and when they are before the prospect they ramble every-which-way. They take 40 minutes and if you had to summarize what they have said it would be very difficult. They waste the golden opportunity they had dreamed of because they don't prepare.

Professional salespeople are willing to do their homework. They know that their persuasive power is directly related to how well prepared they are when they walk in to make a presentation. They research to find out what they need to know about the prospect, they plan what they will show and what they will say, and they practice, practice, practice!

If you want to talk about the Super Bowl, become a sportscaster. If all you want to do is talk about the weather, apply for a job as a weather forecaster. But, if you want to become a powerful persuader, prepare what you will talk about, and what you will do—then do it!

4. *Persuasion-boosting "P" number four is Perform!* Salespeople often complain, "How could that customer buy that over-priced, poorly constructed competitive product? ... He must be an idiot!" It's simple! The complainer was outperformed by a competitive salesperson. People don't buy —they are *sold!* If you don't make a strong presentation, you cannot persuade your prospect to buy.

Powerful persuaders are like stage actors playing to a full-house audience. They have become artists at making their presentations. They are entertaining and informative to watch and hear. When they have finished a presentation, the customer will know all he or she needs to know to make a decision, and that customer will be motivated to do what the salesperson is asking him or her to do.

How much time do you spend on "action time"? Action time is the precious few minutes you have before your prospect actually making your presentation. If you are like most salespeople, you probably spend less than one-third of your time attempting to persuade prospects to buy. You better make it count!

Do you want to add power to your persuasion? Add performance to your presentation! Give every presentation your best shot!

Someone once asked an old master of the piano why he spent several hours a day practicing, when he was already so good. The old master replied, "I wish to become superb!" If you are good at making your presentations, how do you add power to your persuasive skills? You seek to become superb!

5. *If you would boost your selling power, here's the fifth "P" of persuasion: be Perceptive!* The powerful persuaders are alert to everything that happens during a sales interview. They are not preoccupied with personal problems, with airline schedules, or even the next call they are going to make. They realize that reaching a sales goal begins with making *this* sale!

Do you know the four most common reasons people buy? They buy because of *fear,* because of *pride,* because they stand to *gain* something from buying, and they buy because they want to *imitate* others who matter to them. The powerful persuader looks for the motivating force in the prospect's life, and plays to that motivation. By being perceptive to the motivations of a prospect, the professional salesperson appeals to the "hot button" or the key reason that person might buy.

But, it is equally important to know the most common reasons people give for not buying. The number one reason is that they have *no confidence* in either the person selling, the product being sold, or the company represented. The perceptive persuader looks for those hidden meanings that indicate no confidence and seeks to build that confidence. The second reason is, because they feel *no need*. By perceiving this feeling of no need, you can often persuade by showing the need. The third reason people give for not buying is, *no money*. Building value to overcome price objections is a skill of the professional persuader. And, the fourth reason is, that they are in *no hurry*. The powerful persuader gives reasons for buying *now*.

If you would add power to your persuasion, learn to be perceptive. Read your prospects to discover the motivations they have to buy or not to buy.

6. *The sixth "P" of persuasion is Probe.* This subject is so important that we will devote a whole chapter to it later.

The art of asking questions is one of the most important and useful tools of people who become master persuaders.

7. *Seventh on our list of "P's" of persuasion is Personalize.* The most powerful word for selling is the little, three-letter word—"YOU!"

Do you know the primary difference between manipulative and nonmanipulative selling? Manipulative selling is *salesperson-oriented*. It focuses on what the salesperson wants and needs. Nonmanipulative selling is *client-oriented*. It zeroes in on the needs and wants of the prospect.

A person who is looking at the proposition you are offering wants to know just *one* thing: "What's in it for *me*?" Successful real estate salespeople know that a house is not sold until the prospective owners take "psychological control" of that house. They are concerned about the personal needs of their customers and gear everything in their presentations to that magic moment when a client stops calling it a house, and starts to call it a "home."

If you would add power to your persuasion, personalize every part of your presentation to meet your prospect's own personal needs and wants.

8. *The eighth "P" in persuasion is Please.* Powerful persuaders seek to close sales by pleasing their clients. When the prospect becomes happy about the idea of owning what you are selling, that prospect will become a customer.

There's an old saying that you can lead a horse to water but you can't make him drink. To that I would answer, you can put enough salt in his food to make him want to drink. Professional salespeople know that they cannot force their prospects to buy. They seek to please them in so many ways that they create the desire to buy.

9. *Ninth on our list of the "P's" of persuasion is Prove.* Don't make statements you can't back up with facts. And, don't expect your clients to accept at face value everything you say. Be prepared to prove by tests, findings, and performance records *every* claim you make.

One of the best ways to persuade by proving is to give proof statements from people who are happy with your products or services.

Facts are persuasive! Learn to use them, and become a powerful persuader.

10. *Finally, the tenth "P" of persuasion is Persist.* Call on the prospect as many times as you feel is warranted. Listen to this:

- 50% of America's salespeople call on a prospect once and quit.

- 18% of America's salespeople call on a prospect twice and quit.
- 7% of America's salespeople call on a prospect three times and quit.
- 5% of America's salespeople call on a prospect four times and quit.
- But, 20% of America's salespeople call on a prospect five or more times before they quit.

And, did you know that it's this 20% who calls five or more times that closes *80%* of the sales in America!

A sales manager friend of mine used to illustrate persistence this way: "Don't stick your foot in the door, stick your head in the door; if they slam the door on your neck, you can keep on talking!"

PERSUADE WITH POWER!

There they are: *10 ways* to add power to your persuasion, and boost your selling power!

You don't have to become a dynamic personality to sell. You don't have to put pressure on people, or out-talk people to sell. Maybe Robert Browning said it best when he said, "The great mind knows the power of gentleness."

Learn how to persuade more effectively and you can boost your selling power.

* * *

QUESTIONS FOR REVIEW AND APPLICATION

Rate yourself on a scale of 1-10 on each of the following "Ten P's of Persuasion." Then set a plan of action for improving each.

1. Successful salespeople are *positive* in their attitudes about themselves, their companies, and their products or services.

MY RATING: (1 2 3 4 5 6 7 8 9 10)

MY ACTION PLAN: _____

_____

2. Professional salespeople concentrate on *prospects* who can buy, and who have good reasons to buy.

MY RATING: (1 2 3 4 5 6 7 8 9 10)

MY ACTION PLAN: _____

_____

3. Successful salespeople adequately *prepare* before every presentation.

MY RATING: (1 2 3 4 5 6 7 8 9 10)

MY ACTION PLAN: _____

_____

4. Professional salespeople are like stage actors playing to a full-house audience—*They perform.*

MY RATING: (1 2 3 4 5 6 7 8 9 10)

MY ACTION PLAN: _____

_____

5. Successful persuaders are alert to everything that happens during the sales interview—They are *perceptive.*

MY RATING: (1 2 3 4 5 6 7 8 9 10)

MY ACTION PLAN: _____

_____

6. Professional salespeople are masters at asking questions—They *probe.*

MY RATING: (1 2 3 4 5 6 7 8 9 10)

MY ACTION PLAN: _____

---

7. Successful persuaders *personalize* everything in the sales interview to the client's interest.

MY RATING: (1 2 3 4 5 6 7 8 9 10)

MY ACTION PLAN: _____

---

8. Powerful persuaders seek to close sales by *pleasing* their customers.

MY RATING: (1 2 3 4 5 6 7 8 9 10)

MY ACTION PLAN: _____

---

9. Professional salespeople don't make statements and claims they can't back up—They always *prove.*

MY RATING: (1 2 3 4 5 6 7 8 9 10)

MY ACTION PLAN: _____

---

10. Powerful persuaders call on a prospect as many times as they feel is warranted—They are *persistent.*

MY RATING: (1 2 3 4 5 6 7 8 9 10)

MY ACTION PLAN: _____

10.

Raise Your Customer Response Potential

The most important person in the career of a salesperson is the customer.

"It is not the employer who pays wages. Employers only handle the money. It is the customer who pays wages," said Henry Ford. And, we might add, it is the customer who pays commissions.

A young sales clerk in a large department store was in a particularly bad mood one day, and took out all his frustrations on the customers. Most people just put up with the lack of courtesy and inattention they received. Finally, a middle-aged woman stepped up to the counter to see some merchandise.

"Can I help you?" the clerk snarled at her.

"Oh! You've got it all backwards!" the lady replied. "You are *overhead* here; I am *profit!*"

Too many salespeople forget that success is spelled C-U-S-T-O-M-E-R!

CUSTOMER RESPONSE IS THE NAME OF THE GAME!

Bud Wilkinson was one of the most successful coaches in the history of college football. He had a reputation for getting extraordinary performances out of ordinary players. A famous sportswriter went to the University of Oklahoma to try to find out exactly how he was able to motivate those students to play their hearts out.

It was a big game, the stands were full, and the crowd was very vocal about its feelings. When a pass was dropped or a tackle missed, the crowd would "boo" and "hiss" as the offending player made his way off the field.

Then the sportswriter noticed something strange. Oklahoma was down by a touchdown, the crowd was "hissing" and "booing" its displeasure—but the players didn't seem to notice! Instead, when they came off the field, they'd head straight for the coach and say something to him before they went to the bench.

"How can you guys ignore the crowd like that?" he asked one of the players.

"It's the coach who decides who plays next Saturday and we play to the coach, not the crowd!" the player said.

That story contains one of the most vital bits of information a salesperson can ever learn. It is the customer who decides who will make a sale!

If you would raise your customer response potential, *play to the customer!*

You watch the old pros, the *big producers!* Everything they do and everything they say is geared toward *one* person —*the customer!*

As I noted earlier in this book, when I asked seasoned salespeople, "What's the biggest change you've noticed in selling over the years?," most of them give me a two-word answer, "The customer!"

Sometimes they go on to explain that buyers are more professional, that consumers are better educated, that their prospects have been bombarded by sales pitches on television and radio and have cultivated the habit of *tuning out* sales presentations.

So, how do you break through all of that resistance? How do you get that customer to respond favorably to you? How do you get that customer to *act?*

You *individualize* your presentation! You play to each customer as if that customer is the *only* customer you have ever had, and the only person to whom you will ever make a presentation. You make that customer *want* to do business with you!

Sound like a tough assignment? You bet it is! Let me confess, up front, that individualizing presentations is one of the toughest parts of selling I have ever tried to master. But, every effort I have ever put into it has paid off. . . *Big!*

In my estimation, tailoring the sales interview to the customer is what separates the peddlers from the professional salespeople. Peddlers sell products and services; professionals *sell customers*—one customer at a time!

PRINCIPLES THAT WORK

How do you raise your customer response potential by playing to the customer? Since you are an individual, and each customer you play to is an individual, I can only give you a set of principles, or guidelines that you can tailor to fit your own situation.

But, believe me, these principles work! They will help you close more sales, with less effort.

PRINCIPLE #1: People buy from salespeople they trust!

What are the first three questions most prospects ask? They may vary some in the way they're asked but they always boil down to these three questions: Who are you? Whom do you represent? What do you want from me?

Psychologists have taught us a lot about gaining trust by explaining how animals behave when they feel their territories are being invaded. Some animals will run and hide, others will make a lot of noise to try to scare off the invader, and still others will turn and fight. In fact, almost any animal, when it feels sufficiently threatened, will rise up to defend its territory. Sounds like some prospects I've encountered!

The amount of tension usually determines how the animal will react. There are several factors that affect the tension level brought by an invasion: the speed of the invader, the appearance of the invader, the attitude and demeanor of the invader, the manner of the approach, the perceived intent, and the actions of the invader.

People have the same kinds of "comfort zones." Some are emotional "comfort zones," and others are physical "comfort zones." But the result is always the same: invade that "comfort zone," and *tension rises!*

That's why everything the salesperson *says* and *does* will produce either tension or trust. *If I create tension, I get resistance! If I create trust, I get response!*

Some salespeople get all hyped up in a sales meeting and go out to pounce upon their first prospect. They back that customer into a corner, roll up their sleeves, knock down all objections, and *close! close! close!*

No wonder all of us who sell have to work so hard to build trust!

Listen to these comments a very successful old veteran made to a group of new salespeople his company had just hired. He said, "I am a completely free individual, and my customer is a completely free individual! I can drive a dirty, ragged car; I can wear outlandish or wrinkled clothes; I can wear my hair any way I please; I can tell dirty jokes and ethnic stories; I can say exactly anything I feel like saying; I can do *anything* I choose—as long as I recognize that my customer has the right to buy *anything* he chooses, from *anybody* he chooses, *anytime* he chooses! This is a free country!"

What a *powerful* statement! Many excellent books and articles have been written on appearance, sales etiquette, courtesy, being pleasant, and many of the other factors the old veteran alluded to. I find it helpful to review those things almost constantly.

I asked an old pro, "How do you know if you have built trust with a client?" His answer was a classic. He said, "It's like when I want to kiss my wife. . . . When it's right, I know it, and she knows it!"

He went on to say, "I'm sensitive to the customer . . . when he's tense, I do something to ease the tension; when he's comfortable, I move in."

The first principle for raising your customer response potential is this: People buy from salespeople they *trust!* Build trust and get *response!*

PRINCIPLE #2: People buy from salespeople they respect!

One reason I drive an expensive new car is that I don't have time to waste taking it to the shop every day. And when something goes wrong with that car, do I take it to a "shade-tree mechanic" so I can save a buck? *No!* I take that car to a competent, well-qualified mechanic. I take it to a person whose professional skills I respect.

And, boy, is that guy expensive! But he has convinced me that he can always find the trouble and fix my car. He has gained my *respect!*

Now, I trust my banker, but not to fix my car! I trust my attorney, but not to fix my car! I trust my wife, but I don't respect her abilities to fix my car!

You ask a busy parent, or a busy executive for an appointment for a sales interview, and that person asks a very important question. "Why should I spend my *precious* time listening to *this* person?"

When the answer to that question is, "This person has something to say that is important for *me* to *hear*," you've got your appointment.

Bob and Herb Shook talk about the "importance of *being* important," in their great book, *How To Be The Complete Professional Salesman.* They suggest that you look at your own experience to see why you listen to certain salespeople, while you turn others off as "just another salesman." *It's simple, you listen to people you think will have something important to say!*

You look for signs of self-confidence, you look for evidence of success, you look for evidence of respect from other people. And, according to Herb and Bob Shook, your customers look for the same evidences in you. If you look, act, and talk like you have something important to say, people will give you the time to say it.

Once you establish that relationship of respect, it is important to keep it. How do you do that? You keep respect by showing respect.

Here are some tips on how to do that:

1. *Respect the prospect's time, even if the prospect doesn't.* A salesman I know learned a valuable lesson about this. A busy executive spent three hours with him on the first visit. He refused to see the salesman on several later calls. Finally, the salesman asked why, and the executive said, "I have a tendency to talk too much with some people ... and you're *one* of them!"

   Don't be abrupt, or discourteous. Be *businesslike!* Do your business as quickly as you can, and when your business is finished, *leave!*

2. *Respect the prospect's territory!* Remember, you're a guest—act like one!

3. *Respect the prospect's intelligence!* Sometimes you can gain entrance by trickery, but you won't gain respect.

   People respect salespeople who are competent, self-confident, successful, and who show respect for them. People buy from salespeople they *respect.*

PRINCIPLE #3: People want to make their own decisions!

If they respect a salesperson they will welcome information from that salesperson. They will even seek the advice of a salesperson they trust; but, when it's time to sign on the dotted line, they want to feel that the decision made is theirs.

Professional salespeople don't try to impose their decisions on a client; they try to help that person reach his or her own decision. They use nonmanipulative sales techniques.

Their sales interviews are client-oriented rather than salesperson-oriented: they seek to discover needs rather than to create needs; they discuss with their clients rather than talk *at* them; they are adaptable and flexible. They offer ideas and suggest solutions rather than use terms like, "You're foolish if you don't take this offer," or, "Take it or leave it!"

When a decision favorable to the salesperson is reached, the professional seeks to reinforce that decision with positive comments. And, when the decision is unfavorable to the salesperson, the professional will try to gently move the person by offering new information and suggesting alternative solutions. He tries to lead the client, not push the product.

People want to make their own decisions, and salespeople who help them make their own decisions find that their customer response potential rises steadily.

PRINCIPLE #4: People buy for their reasons, not yours!

When you are in bad need of a commission check, or you are working like crazy to meet your quota, it is sometimes easy to exert undue pressure on the customer, or to beg for an order. Such practices have no place in professional selling.

Most customers couldn't care less if you win a trip to Hawaii, or a "Pac-Man" game, or if you desperately need an order. Their concern is that they get the benefits they want, for the money they are willing to pay.

Contests, quotas, and incentives are designed to stimulate salespeople to work harder and more effectively, not to give you a wedge to use to separate the customer from his or her money.

Some salespeople talk a lot about their own needs and desires, and with some success. However, more often than not, their customers feel manipulated and some even resent it.

"Never make your appeal to a man's better nature; he may not have one," said Lazarus Long, the wise old prophet of science fiction. "Always make your appeal to his self-interest."

That is excellent advice for selling! The greatest way to raise your customer response potential is to be guided by the customer's best interests. If the customer's reason for buying is overwhelming, you've got your sale; if it is not, it matters little what's in it for you, the customer won't buy.

PRINCIPLE #5: People buy from salespeople who understand them and understand their needs and problems.

It makes very little difference how the salesperson perceives the needs and problems of a prospect. What counts is the way the *prospect* sees those needs.

The secret to closing many sales is to help the customer discover the real need behind the expressed need. When a customer says, "I don't need life insurance!" it is seldom helpful to say, "*Everybody* needs life insurance!" It is much more productive to help that customer explore needs that life insurance could meet.

Moving a prospect from "I don't *need* it" to "I'll *take* it" is seldom accomplished by bombardment with all of the wonderful features of a product. More often it is accomplished by helping the customer discover how the product or service will meet needs that person didn't even know he or she had.

Professional salespeople seek first to understand the needs, desires, and problems of their customers and secondly, they seek to help those customers *understand* their needs. Then, and *only* then, do they seek to help their customers discover how what they are selling will meet their needs.

Remember, when you help a person discover what he or she wants and how to get it through what you're selling, your customer response potential will zoom *upward*.

RAISE YOUR CUSTOMER RESPONSE POTENTIAL: RAISE YOUR INCOME!

As a salesperson, you are *overhead,* the customer is *profit!*

Remember, when you open a sales interview, you are invading the customer's "comfort zone." Your success in selling will be directly proportional to your ability to gain the trust, respect, and positive response of that customer. That can best be done by gearing everything you do and everything you say to the customer. *Mostly it is the customer who decides who will make a sale.*

* * *

REVIEW AND APPLICATION

Here is a list of the five principles for playing to the customer. As you review each, do the exercise which follows it. The care with which you approach them could have a direct bearing on how much you are able to raise your customer response potential.

PRINCIPLE #1

People buy from salespeople they trust. List five ways you seek to build trust and reduce the tension level when you call on a new prospect:

1. _____
2. _____
3. _____
4. _____
5. _____

PRINCIPLE #2

People buy from people they respect. List five reasons you will listen to some salespeople, while you simply "tune out" others. As you list them, think about how you can use the five reasons to get your customers to listen to you:

1. _____
2. _____
3. _____
4. _____
5. _____

PRINCIPLE #3

People want to make their own decisions. List, below, three statements that are manipulative (statements that try to force the customer to act) and three statements that are nonmanipulative (statements that allow the customer to make the decision.)

MANIPULATIVE STATEMENTS:

1. _____
2. _____
3. _____

NONMANIPULATIVE STATEMENTS:

1. _____
2. _____
3. _____

PRINCIPLE #4

People buy for their own reasons, not yours. Can you think of a sales interview in which you allowed your own reasons for the customer to buy to color your presentation or close? If not, pat yourself on the back, and go on to the next principle. If so, answer the following questions:

1. What need did you feel? _____

_____

2. What did it cause you to say or do? _____

_____

3. What was the customer's response? _____

_____

4. How can you avoid the problem in the future?

_____

_____

PRINCIPLE #5

People buy from salespeople who understand them, and understand their needs and problems. List three examples of how you have closed a sale by helping a customer discover his or her needs:

1. The Customer: _____
   The Need: _____
   _____

   How I Helped the Customer Discover the Need:
   _____
   _____

2. The Customer: _____
   The Need: _____
   _____

   How I Helped the Customer Discover the Need:
   _____
   _____

3. The Customer: _____
   The Need: _____
   _____

   How I Helped the Customer Discover the Need:
   _____
   _____

11.

Have You Discovered The Power Of Asking Questions?

Have you discovered the tremendous selling power of asking questions? Or, are you still killing sales by concentrating on positive statements?

Have you ever thought about why asking questions is such a powerful selling tool? Is it because it gives the customer an opportunity to get involved in the selling situation? Or, is it because it provides you with the information you need to know to close the sale?

Do you realize how much information can be conveyed, simply by asking questions?

But, isn't it frustrating for someone to ask questions in rapid succession, without giving you an opportunity to respond? Of course it is! Why? Becuase asking questions is the greatest single tool you can use to get people to respond to you!

The artful asking of questions is the best way to raise your customer response potential. And, isn't that what selling is all about?

To be sure, the wrong questions can cause a person to react negatively to you. Even the right questions, asked in the wrong way, or at the wrong time, can frighten a prospect away.

I once heard about a barber who was converted after a hell fire and damnation sermon. The next day, he wanted to convert all of his customers. He lathered up the face of his first customer, stroked his straight razor on his honing strop, put the razor to his customer's throat and asked, "Are you prepared to meet God?" No wonder the fellow jumped up and ran out of the barbershop, with lather on his face! There's a right time, and a right place, and a right way to ask questions. And, that was none of them.

MANY SMALL DECISIONS

Think about it a minute! Aren't most successful sales made through a series of small positive responses?

Sure, there are exceptions—like the electronics equipment salesman who went to see the purchasing agent of a large aircraft manufacturing company one day. He was a very aggressive person so he launched into his high-powered presentation on the fine performance of the components his company made. He talked so fast the purchasing agent couldn't stop him. Finally, his first question of the interview was an alternate close: "Would you like to read the test results on this new component, or would you like to order one to use to conduct your own tests?" The purchasing agent thought for a moment, then picked up a purchase order he had prepared before the salesman came in, and said, "Send me six of the components!"

That salesman was delighted! But, later he realized that he had not sold anything—the customer had bought! He turned pale with fright when he realized how close he had come to blowing a big order. The purchasing agent had already read the test results. By suggesting the customer order one, and do his own tests, he had almost cancelled out the decision to buy six.

Fast-talking, positive-statement salespeople are often a little like the surgeon who wrote on a patient's chart, "The operation was a success—but the patient died!" Who cares that an appendix was removed successfully if the patient died in the operating room? And, what's the value of a great pitch that doesn't lead to a sale?

The proper questions, artfully asked, set up a series of positive responses that lead to a sale.

WHY ARE QUESTIONS SUCH A POWERFUL TOOL?

Why are questions such a powerful tool for raising your customer response level? Here are only a few of the many important reasons:

First, they can help you *discover important information* that can help you lead the sale to a successful close. You might discover that the person to whom you're talking is not the person to whom the pitch should be made. By asking questions you can discover the key issue, or the real concern of the client. Through probing, you can often discover the hidden objections, or the hidden motivations of the customer.

Secondly, through carefully posed questions, you can *help the prospect make some useful discoveries.* Someone says, "I don't believe in life insurance," and the skilled prober asks, "Why?" By pursuing a line of self-revealing questions, the prospect discovers he really doesn't believe a statement he has used to quickly dismiss every life insurance salesperson he's seen during the last five years.

Thirdly, asking questions, and actively listening to responses, *demonstrates a genuine interest in the customer.* It gets you involved with your prospect. It creates trust and reduces tension, if it's done with real sincerity! It changes your position from invader to guest.

Fourthly, asking questions *gets the prospect involved with you.* It makes him or her an active participant in the sales interview. Conversational selling actually lets the customer help you sell.

Fifthly, when you ask questions, you create the opportunity to discover and correct misconceptions you might have about the client, and erroneous information the client might have received.

And, *finally*, through two-way communication, you can *monitor the tension level and test the bond of trust* between you and the client. Dialogue helps you time all elements of the presentation and the close.

GUARD AGAINST DANGERS

But, aren't there some dangers in asking questions? You bet there are! That's why I keep talking about the question-asking technique as an art.

Let's look at the three big dangers of asking questions in a sales interview—particularly with a new prospect.

DANGER #1: Questions can sometimes offend or frighten off the client.

The barber we talked about earlier wanted to sell his customer on his new-found religious faith, but the questions he asked frightened the poor fellow and made him run off.

People often feel manipulated, or set-up by a salesperson's questions. Have you ever had one of those telephone salespeople who leads off with a question like, "Mr. Jones, do you love your children?" It makes you feel like responding, "No! I hate the little brats!"

And what about those salespeople who ask questions that are too personal, like, "Mrs. Smith, what time will your husband be home?" Mrs. Smith might be afraid she's talking to a rapist who preys on women when their husbands are gone.

The skillful salesperson seeks to build trust by respecting the prospect's intelligence, feelings, and concerns, and by constantly monitoring the tension-trust level.

DANGER #2: Questions can lead the talkative person off on a tangent.

As a result, time runs out before the salesperson gets to first base.

You've seen the type, haven't you? Ask them the time, and they tell you how to make a watch, or about their latest trip to Switzerland.

Interestingly, this danger contains its own solution. In fact, some people are so talkative that they go off on a tangent after a positive statement has been made. Carefully asked questions can be one of the best tools for directing a conversation. The real pros become so good at it that the talkative client never notices that he's being led.

The key to carefully asked questions is to use the client's comments to steer the conversation back to the key issue. For example, "Mr. Brown, I can see that you enjoy travel. Wouldn't you enjoy it more if you knew your possessions were adequately protected?" A person selling burglar alarms could direct that answer right into a close.

DANGER #3: Questions can reinforce negative feelings.

Set a pessimist off with a question about the economy, and that pessimist will get so worked up he'll never buy anything.

Questions that lead a person to talk about deeply personal problems, or politics, or religion, or race can cause your prospect to get so involved with negative feelings that it will be hard to steer the sales interview back to a positive vein.

Of course, positive statements can trigger negative feelings, as can the wrong questions. But, questions are designed to get the prospect talking, and the more that prospect talks, the greater the tendency for deep negative feelings to come out.

Here are some pointers I have found helpful:

1. Choose carefully the types of questions you will ask.

2. Steer clear of explosive subjects like race, religion, politics, and deep personal problem areas.

3. Phrase questions so that they will bring out a positive answer.

4. Focus on the solutions to problems, rather than the problems.

Ask questions that move the prospect toward positive actions aimed at solving the problem with the purchase of your product or service.

The dangers of asking questions can be avoided, and when asking questions is skillfully done, it becomes a tremendous aid in selling.

THE EFFECTIVE USE OF QUESTIONS

How do you ask questions to boost your customer response level?

Here are some guidelines that have been tested thoroughly and proven effective by topflight salespeople in all fields.

GUIDELINE #1: Start with broad questions and move toward more narrow questions.

Open-ended questions are less threatening at the beginning of an interview, when the bond of trust has not yet been fully established.

"Tell me a little about your decorating motif?" That's the kind of question that might start a customer talking about her general needs for furniture or accessories. It can be a very revealing way to start the conversation. If she is proud of what she has, it opens the door for her to brag. If she's frustrated with her decor, she can express her need for a number of items she is considering.

As confidence builds, and the sales interview takes on direction, move in with closed-end questions like, "Do you think the smaller china will fit better into your limited space?"

GUIDELINE #2: Ask—then shut up and listen!

The customer can't talk while you're talking. And, you don't learn while you're talking. Don't just get quiet and try to think up what you're going to say next—listen to every word the prospect says!

GUIDELINE #3: Keep questions simple and focused!

Use one idea at a time. Pursue each topic to its logical conclusion. Target your questions.

GUIDELINE #4: Ask sensitive questions in a nonthreatening way!

"How much were you planning to spend on a car?" is better than, "How much can you afford to put into a car?" Explain why, if you must ask a sensitive question. People will answer even touchy questions if they understand why they are asked. Always explain why if you must ask a very personal question.

GUIDELINE #5: Always ask questions that are easy to answer!

Studies show that people would rather answer a question when they agree, than to voice their objections. As you observe the customer, and listen to that customer's comments, you can sense the customer's moods. As you do this, you can ask a series of questions that can be answered by "yes," or at least in agreement.

GUIDELINE #6: Turn the statements your customer makes into questions to clarify or reinforce feelings.

"So Tuesday would be best for you, is that right?" With that question you have clarified the day the customer seems to prefer.

When a prospect expresses a strong feeling, reinforce it with a question. "If I hear you right, you're saying that your clients don't have time to fill out long forms?" That lets your customer know that you really heard what was said, and gives an opportunity for him or her to elaborate.

GUIDELINE #7: Use questions to develop the presentation!

"You mentioned that your present car needs repair. What kind of repairs does it need?" By asking that type of question, you can move toward explaining the advantages of a new car.

GUIDELINE #8: Use caution when leading clients with questions.

Professional buyers and many consumers have become sophisticated enough to realize when they are being "set up for the kill," and often they will resent it. Always respect the intelligence of your prospect!

GUIDELINE #9: Use questions to give information.

It is amazing how much information can be conveyed, and how many opinions expressed, through questions. Do you recall that series of questions I asked at the beginning of this chapter? You might find it interesting to go back and notice how many opinions and how much information I packed into those first seven sentences. Yet, every one of them was a question.

ARE YOU ASKING ENOUGH QUESTIONS?

The skillful asking of questions is the best way to raise your customer response potential. Most sales are the result of a series of small commitments and affirmative answers, rather than a single big "yes."

If you would improve your customer response level, master the art of asking questions. But, remember: Always allow your customer to answer each question and listen, really listen, while the customer is talking.

People love to hear themselves talk. If you learn how to skillfully provide them that opportunity by asking questions, they will reward you with answers you can take to the bank.

* * *

QUESTIONS FOR REVIEW AND APPLICATION

Are you asking as many of the right kinds of questions as you should be asking? In each of the areas below, we will give you an opportunity to respond. Don't you think it would be helpful for you to think about each response as you check it off?

REASONS QUESTIONS ARE HELPFUL

1. Have you been able to gain valuable information that can help you close sales by asking questions?

    YES ( )   NO ( )

2. Do you help your prospects make useful discoveries by asking questions?

    YES ( )   NO ( )

3. Do you show your prospects you are interested by asking questions and then listening to their responses?

    YES ( )   NO ( )

4. Can you see how asking questions gets your prospect involved as an active participant in the presentation?

    YES ( )   NO ( )

5. Do you seek to discover and correct misconceptions through asking questions?

        YES ( )   NO ( )

6. Do you use two-way communications to monitor the trust level with your prospects?

        YES ( )   NO ( )

DANGERS OF ASKING QUESTIONS

1. Do you seek to avoid offending or frightening off a prospect by the use of questions that are too personal or make the prospect feel "set up"?

        YES ( )   NO ( )

2. Do you try to control the talkative prospect by asking questions that lead back to the key issue?

        YES ( )   NO ( )

3. Do you avoid asking questions about race, religion, or politics—or other questions that can reinforce negative feelings?

        YES ( )   NO ( )

GUIDELINES FOR EFFECTIVE QUESTIONS

1. Do you start with broad questions and move toward more narrow questions?

        YES ( )   NO ( )

2. Do you shut up and listen after you have asked a question?

        YES ( )   NO ( )

3. Do you keep questions simple and focused?

   YES ( )   NO ( )

4. Do you always ask questions that are easy for the prospect to answer in the affirmative?

   YES ( )   NO ( )

5. Do you turn the statements your customer makes into questions to clarify or reinforce feelings?

   YES ( )   NO ( )

6. Do you use questions to develop the presentation along the lines of the prospect's interests?

   YES ( )   NO ( )

7. Do you use caution to avoid making the prospect feel "set up for the kill" in your use of questions?

   YES ( )   NO ( )

8. Have you discovered how much information can be conveyed through questions?

   YES ( )   NO ( )

12.

Put Power In Your Presentation

I want to give you what some of my corporate clients call "The Nido Qubein method of putting power in a presentation." It's KISMIF! You don't recognize the word?

Don't look for it in your dictionary; it isn't there!

It is an acronym made up of six letters—K-I-S-M-I-F.

Those letters stand for Keep It Simple—Make It Fun! Want to put power in your presentation? Keep it simple and make it fun!

I asked one salesman what was the last thing he did in every presentation. He said, "I wake up my prospect." No wonder he had to be *sent* to a seminar for *help!*

How do you keep every presentation simple, and make every presentation *fun?* Those who do it *best* approach *every* presentation as if it were a major stage production. In fact, some salespeople I've seen would make terrific actors, producers, and writers.

FOUR TARGETS FOR EACH PRESENTATION

Professional salespeople have four targets in mind for every presentation they make.

First, they plan to get an order! Now, they can't always deliver a hundred percent on that goal, but they can, and do, score a bullseye on each of the next three goals.

Secondly, they want to make sure the person *understands* and desires what they have to offer.

Thirdly, they make sure the prospect *enjoys* the time they spend together.

And, *finally,* they make certain the prospect has had an opportunity to *buy.*

Very successful salespeople have learned that the more of the last three targets they hit, the more they hit the *first* target—*getting an order.*

Have you ever had a prospect say to you, "I enjoyed that presentation"? Professional buyers are often so jaded by all of the sales interviews they sit through that it's *hard to impress them*—but the professional *tries,* and *tries hard!* And consumers have seen big stars, big sets, and powerful writing in television commercials so often that it's sometimes hard to get their attention. But those salespeople who are successful always give it their *best shot.*

Sure, you can't fly through airports, like O.J. Simpson, but even "The Juice" can't look your prospect square in the eyes, he can't *listen* to your prospect's needs and desires, and he can't *observe* every move the prospect makes. So, you've got some advantages! Use them!

Almost everybody enjoys seeing almost anybody do almost anything really well! Do you remember that Pepsi commercial in which the little girl was learning how to twirl a baton? Now, I've never been very excited by little girls twirling batons, but when she was in that parade, and everybody was looking at her, I found myself pulling for her like crazy! I let out a sigh of relief when she caught that baton! I wanted to see her succeed!

Put a little *ham* in your presentation! Your customers will *love* it!

POWER-PACKING STRATEGIES

How do you add life to your presentations? Top performers have found that there are at least eight strategies that help.

STRATEGY #1: Prepare your presentation in advance!

There's an old story about a young minister who preached his first sermon in his home church. After the service, he asked his grandmother how he had done. Now Grandmother always told the truth, so the young man was thrilled when she said, "I only saw three things wrong with it." He asked her to tell him the three flaws she saw in his very first sermon, and the grandmother replied, "First, you *read* it; secondly, you read it *poorly*; and thirdly, it wasn't *worth reading!*"

I won't ask you if you ever had a presentation that had those three things wrong with it. I certainly have! And, from those poor presentations I learned the *value* of *preparation*.

If you are like most salespeople, you only have a *few* hours a day in front of customers, presenting your products. That time is so valuable that you have to make it *count!*

How do you prepare your presentation for maximum effectiveness?

Step #1: Select the materials you will use. Make a complete list of everything you think is necessary to sell your customer.

Step #2: Write out every single word you will use in presenting each bit of information you will offer. Use strong selling words like: proven, easy, guarantee, results, comfort, proud, profit, new, trust, value, and vital. Keep rewriting and paring it down until you can say all that you want to say briefly and with power.

Step #3: Organize the presentation by connecting the various parts so that they will flow in a logical sequence.

Step #4: Gather and refine all of the sales aids and sales literature you will use.

STRATEGY #2: Prepare yourself for the presentation!

It doesn't matter if you have called on the prospect a dozen times. You need to be ready to do your best *every* time you walk in to see that prospect.

Practice that presentation! If you have available a videotape machine and camera, that can help a great deal. Record your presentation; then play it back and critique it. Keep repeating that process until you are satisfied with the way it looks. Then, get somebody else to critique it. If you don't have a videotape recorder, stand in front of a mirror and record on an audio cassette player.

Practice on your wife, or your husband, or a friendly neighbor, or trade practices with a fellow-salesperson. Drill, drill, drill until you can do it in your sleep!

There's an old cop-out that costs many salespeople a lot of money. "I don't use canned presentations!" they will tell you. Most of them ramble all over the place and waste valuable *time* and beautiful *opportunities*. It doesn't matter if you use it word-for-word; if you know it thoroughly, you are more likely to get everything in. Perhaps even more importantly, if you know that presentation like the back of your hand, you will be free to concentrate all of your mental energies on the sales interview.

Even the greatest public speakers—people who have been doing it for decades and always speak extemporaneously—practice every part of their speech they think they might need to use.

Once you have practiced thoroughly, work on your attitude. *Enthusiasm* is one of the greatest assets a salesperson can cultivate. One great salesman shared how he enrolled in a public speaking course to learn how to communicate more effectively. As he was making his first public speech, his instructor, who happened to be Dale Carnegie, *stopped* him.

"Do you *believe* what you are saying? Does it *matter* to you?" he asked the young salesman.

"Sure, I believe it!" he replied.

Then Mr. Carnegie said, "Put some *enthusiasm* into it—*make us believe it!*" I learned a long time ago that if I am not enthusiastic about what I'm saying, it is impossible to get anybody else enthusiastic about it.

Practice, and get excited about your presentation!

STRATEGY #3: Set the stage for maximum advantage!

Too often, you will have to perform the best you can in the setting available.

But, if you have anything to say about it, try to get to a quiet place, where there are as few distractions as possible. As a matter of fact, if you ask your customer if you could move to a quieter place, that request will often be granted—particularly if the prospect feels you have something important to say.

A good rule of thumb is to always head for the best spot you can possibly get to make your presentations.

STRATEGY #4: Get the customer's attention!

Don't *start* that presentation until you have found that point of contact with the customer. Practice looking the customer straight in the eye with a warm friendly look, and wait until that customer looks into your eyes.

Do something dramatic, but be careful! I heard about a salesman in the old days who went into a prospect's house and sprinkled dirt all over her carpet. "I'll eat my hat if this vacuum cleaner won't pick up that dirt!" he proudly announced. His customer smiled and said, "I hope you brought some ketchup and mustard, 'cause we don't have electricity!" He did something dramatic, but not very wise.

A good ploy is to pick out something in the prospect's environment that indicates a strong interest and use that as a point of contact. Or, ask a question that will involve your prospect.

Concentrate on getting attention, *before* you start the presentation.

STRATEGY #5: Speak clearly and distinctly!

Use a pleasant but confident tone. Make it obvious that you know what you want to say, that you think it is important for the client to hear, and that you are excited about saying it.

Use common words. Avoid jargon or trade slang that might confuse the prospect. Remember, you are expected to know much more about your product or service than the client does. You are not there to impress that customer with what you know, but what the product will do for *him* or *her*.

STRATEGY #6: Get the prospect involved and keep the prospect involved!

If you are selling chairs, invite the prospect to sit down. If it's mattresses, get the prospect to *lie* down. Get the product in the consumer's hand, or under his feet; get her to hold a fabric swatch. Look for any reasonable way to get the prospect involved.

The more involved the prospect is, the more that prospect will help you sell.

By all means, remember what we said about asking questions. Draw the prospect into the conversation.

Another tip I have learned from the exciting salespeople I have known is: Make your presentation *animated!* Move around, use your *hands*, concentrate on *facial expressions*. Try to get the prospect to become animated.

STRATEGY #7: Use props!

Simple, well-designed sales aids can do for the salesperson what stage props do for the actor.

The best props are designed to make a client see, or feel, the benefit of owning a product or buying a service. With a little imagination, almost any product or service can be better shown with props than described with words.

Remember, people learn about seven times as much through their eyes as they do their ears. And, if you can get people to *do* something, they get much more involved in it than if you just describe it for them.

Keep all sales aids *simple*. One outstanding sales manager I know invests a great deal of time and energy in teaching his salespeople how to talk with a pencil. There's more to it than just *doodling;* carefully planned *marks,* strategically made, can draw a customer *into* a presentation. Anybody will watch a pencil at work! It's even more effective if you can make the prospect do the writing or make the marks.

By all means, make sure the props will work, and practice using them until you are very comfortable with them. There is nothing as devastating as a prop that goes wrong during a demonstration, or forgetting how to *operate* a prop. If you are talking about how quietly a machine will run, by all means make sure it's not damaged in transit so that it sounds like a threshing machine when you plug it in.

A good rule of thumb for using props effectively is: Always reinforce every major point of the presentation with sales literature, a sample, or a demonstration that *drives home* the point.

GIVE 'EM A SHOW THEY WON'T FORGET!

Remember, there is a lot of competition out there. Your presentations need everything you can put into them to make them exciting to *hear,* to *watch,* to *experience!*

When a prospect sets aside part of a busy day to give us a few minutes to put on our show, that's a *very big compliment* to us as salespeople. The most productive thing we can do to show our appreciation is to *give them a show they won't forget!*

"When you do what it is you do so well that people who see you do it will want to see you do it again, and will bring others to see you do it, you can have unlimited abundance," someone has said. Nowhere is that more true than in sales presentations.

* * *

REVIEW AND APPLICATION

We are going to list the strategies we suggested for making each presentation a major production. After each one, develop a new tactic for implementing that strategy:

STRATEGY #1

Prepare your presentation in advance! Select all the materials you will need, write out your presentation, organize the presentation so that it flows smoothly, gather and refine all the sales aids you plan to use, and arrange everything for easy access.

MY NEW TACTIC: _____

_____

STRATEGY #2

Prepare yourself for the presentation! Practice, practice, practice, build enthusiasm, and get excited about your presentation.

MY NEW TACTIC: _____

_____

STRATEGY #3

Set the stage for maximum advantage! Always try to get the best spot (good lighting, few distractions, no interruptions, etc.) you can possibly get for your presentation.

MY NEW TACTIC: _____

STRATEGY #4

Get the customer's attention before you start, and keep it! Don't start the presentation until you have found the "point of contact" with the customer.

MY NEW TACTIC: _____

STRATEGY #5

Speak clearly and distinctly! Use a pleasant, but confident, tone of voice; use common words and simple illustrations.

MY NEW TACTIC: _____

STRATEGY #6

Get the prospect involved and keep the prospect involved! Ask questions, ask the customer to do something, be animated in your gestures and facial expressions, use sales aids and samples.

MY NEW TACTIC: _____

STRATEGY #7

Use props! Simple, well-designed sales aids can help the client see and feel what you are talking about. They can involve the client. Always reinforce every major point with a sample, a demonstration, or sales literature.

MY NEW TACTIC: _____

_____

13.

Focus For Maximum Effect

When I was a little boy, my brother gave me a small magnifying glass. It didn't take me long to learn that that little piece of glass contained a secret that gave it tremendous power.

If I would hold the little glass between an object and the sun, and focus it just right, soon it would burn a hole in the object. When it was adjusted exactly right, it would focus all of the sun's energy onto one tiny spot, and intensify the power of the sun by many times. I'm sure you made the same discovery.

That little trick of focussing the sun's rays onto a single spot opened up a whole new game for me. In one sunny day, I burned my initials into every piece of wood in my yard.

TARGETED POWER IS CONCENTRATED POWER

But I learned something far more valuable from that discovery than how to create holes. I learned the tremendous power of concentration—the power of focus—the power of targeting! And nothing can add more power to your presentation than focussing all your energies toward a limited set of targets.

TARGET #1: Target the customer!

We need to develop the importance of playing everything in the preparation and presentation to the customer.

People buy from those salespeople who help them discover what they want and how they can get it through their products and services.

If there is one master key to unlocking the sale, it is to sell benefits. Remember this, the customer always wants to know, "What's in it for me?"

All of the design, engineering, manufacturing, and management skills of your company amount to nothing unless you can show the customer how the product or service will benefit him or her!

One successful salesperson I know explains her technique for targeting the customer like this. She says, "I always pretend that the product was designed specifically for that customer, that it was built exclusively for that customer, and that today is the day of the great unveiling of that product for that single person." That's targeting!

Most sales are made one at a time, to one person at a time. To do that we must ask every question, make every statement, demonstrate each feature and benefit to the one person to whom we are talking at the moment.

TARGET #2: Target the key issue!

As you ask questions and listen closely to the answers, and as you observe the customer, usually one major concern or interest will stand out above all the rest.

Call it the major problem, call it the point of interest, call it the most obvious desire—it all boils down to one thing. What interests that prospect most? Whatever it is, let that be the primary focus of your entire presentation and close.

If that prospect wants to talk savings, talk savings. If that prospect is most interested in making a profit, talk profits that can be made by using your product or service. If that consumer is most interested in convenience, demonstrate every feature that product has to make everything more convenient for him or her. And then, take it one step further, make it as convenient as possible to purchase that product.

J.P. Morgan was one of America's greatest financiers because he understood what motivates people. Mr. Morgan once said, "There are always two reasons people have for doing everything: the reason they state, and the real reason." Discovering that real reason for doing things is one of the most important tasks of making a presentation.

For example, a person may say he needs a new car because the old one gets low mileage. But economy might not be the key issue. As you probe, and observe, you might discover that the real reason the person is interested in a new car is that his neighbor just bought one.

Hesitance to buy might be due to the fact that the customer is satisfied with the service another company is giving. As you probe more deeply you might discover that the customer is upset with someone in your company. Until that key issue is satisfactorily dealt with, it is doubtful you will be able to sell that customer anything.

Remember, there are four basic reasons people buy. People buy out of fear; people buy because of pride of ownership; people buy because of something they stand to gain from the product or service; and people buy to imitate others whom they respect. Memorize those four things because one of those four things is most likely to be the key issue towards which you will want to target your presentation. Be on the alert for fear, for pride, for a desire for gain, and for a desire to imitate.

Now, do you remember the four main reasons people don't buy? These, too, can be key issues. If you recognize any one of these as the customer's key concern, you can focus most of the attention of the presentation to deal with the key objection. The four primary reasons people don't buy are: they don't have confidence in the salesperson, the company, or the product; they don't have a need for the product or service; the cost is too great; or they are not in a hurry.

I'm going to show you exactly how to deal with each of those reasons in the chapter on handling objections. But it is important that you watch out for each of them during your entire presentation. The customer might say, "I don't want your product because your price is too high," but the real reason is that one of your products performed poorly, and was not serviced satisfactorily. Until that issue is dealt with, you are wasting your time. Deal with the no-confidence problem, and you can get the presentation back on the track.

There are two reasons people buy, or don't buy products —the reason they tell you, and the real reason. Learn to focus the key issue, and direct all of the energy of the presentation to deal with that issue, and you will put power in your presentation.

TARGET #3: Target the "hot button!"

What does your customer like about your product? Discover that as early as you can, then focus as much attention as possible on that one exciting feature.

If you're selling cars, and your customer falls in love with the beautiful interior of the demonstrator, don't waste a

Focus For Maximum Effect

lot of time explaining the advanced suspension system. Focus your attention on the "hot button."

If you are calling on a furniture store, and the buyer thinks his customers will like the styling of your products, present everything you can to reinforce that feeling. Help that customer imagine people coming into the store and fighting over your designs.

It's called building value! You start with the primary point of excitement, and you enhance that excitement in every way you can. Then, you add on the other features and benefits that supplement the primary point of interest.

Some successful salespeople like to think of targeting the "hot button" as finding the most vulnerable point. They zero-in on the customer's weakest point of resistance.

Perhaps a more positive approach is to take what is most exciting about the product to a particular customer, and make that the strongest part of your presentation.

Some of the best salespeople in America are the people who make television commercials for major companies. They use the term "your unique selling proposition." Since they have only 30 seconds to make their presentation, they focus everything to that unique selling proposition. They concentrate on the one reason most people buy a product. Think about that the next time somebody asks you, "How do you spell relief?"

Target your customer's primary point of interest in your product and you can focus your presentation for maximum effect.

TARGET #4: Target your timing!

Every good presentation is a masterpiece of timing. It starts with showing up exactly on time, or a few minutes early for the presentation. This says to the customer that you think his or her time is valuable.

Next, you get to the point as quickly as you can, without being abrupt. Of course, you want to establish contact, but as soon as that is done, get down to business!

Listen, observe, and monitor the trust level so that you can move to the next point of your presentation at precisely the right time. This takes practice, but just because you make a lot of presentations, don't think it will come automatically. You have to cultivate a sensitivity to every mood change, every signal the customer sends.

Remember the comment of the old pro—"It's like when I want to kiss my wife—when it's right, I'll know it and she'll know it!"

Listen carefully to your favorite comedian sometime. That performer will time every joke, every punch line, every pause exactly right to get the maximum impact.

And, by all means, end your presentation on time. If you have been promised 15 minutes, finish your presentation in 15 minutes or less. If the customer invites you to stay, or begins to ask questions about the product, don't rush out. But don't overstay your welcome.

The most useful tool of timing is the art of brevity—learning how to say what you want to say in the shortest possible time to be effective. Wordy salespeople might do well to remember that the writer of Genesis told the whole story of the creation of the world in just 442 words. Now that's brevity!

Cultivate a client-oriented sense of timing and you can increase the power of your presentations.

TARGET #5: Target your answer to every question the customer asks!

One of the best ways to build trust is to give a definite, direct answer to every question the customer asks.

If you have studied your products and services, you should have the answer right at the tip of your fingers. If you don't know the answer, promise to get it right away, then follow up immediately with the information requested.

It might cause you to rearrange your presentation to answer a question about price before you are ready, but not nearly as much as having to totally re-establish the trust-bond that has been broken by an evasive answer. Evasiveness creates tension, and usually comes back to haunt you when you're ready to close.

When you think a direct answer might be misleading and damaging, go ahead and give the answer, and then explain why you think it is misleading.

TARGET #6: Target your facts!

Sometimes we get so excited and so enthusiastic about our products and services that we tend to exaggerate about the wonders of what we are selling.

One old salesman was in trouble with his company and his customers almost constantly because he would promise people anything to get a sale. His sales manager chewed him out about it, and the salesman said, "You know, I've cried a bathtub of tears over that habit!" He still didn't get the message.

Professional salespeople, who've been at it for a long time, say that the best rule is to never tell a lie. Sooner or later, those little misrepresentations always come back to haunt you. Better to lose a few sales by telling the truth, than to gain the reputation of one who cannot be trusted.

Target your facts! Don't make claims and promises you can't back up.

TARGET FOR POWER

Put power in your presentation by targeting your customer, your key issue, the customer's "hot button," your timing, your answers, and your facts.

When you focus all of your attention on the most important factors in a presentation, you can concentrate all of your energies where they will do the most good. When you learn how to do that as a professional salesperson, just like that little magnifying glass I talked about, you can burn a hole in the customer's resistance.

Targeted power is concentrated power, and concentrated power leads to more sales.

* * *

TARGETING THE TARGETS

If you would like to present your sales talk with power, memorize the six targets, and concentrate on them in each presentation. To help you get them fixed clearly in your mind, we will review each and give you an opportunity to write out what each target means to you.

TARGET #1

Target the customer! Since the customer always wants to know, "What's in it for me?" *sell benefits.* Talk only to the customer you are before, and speak only to the interests of that customer.

WHAT THIS TARGET MEANS TO ME: _____

_____

_____

TARGET #2

Target the key issue! As you listen and observe, one major concern or point of interest will stand out above all the rest. Target your entire presentation to settle that key issue.

WHAT THIS TARGET MEANS TO ME: _____

_____

_____

TARGET #3

Target the "hot button!" What one feature or benefit does your prospect like best about your product or service? Build value by focussing your attention on the thing your prospect likes most.

WHAT THIS TARGET MEANS TO ME: _____

_____

_____

TARGET #4

Target your timing! Show up on time for the presentation, get to the point quickly, monitor the trust level throughout the interview, watch for buying signals, and end the interview on time. The greatest aid to timing is brevity.

WHAT THIS TARGET MEANS TO ME: _____

_____

_____

TARGET #5

Target your answer to every question the customer asks! To build trust, give a definite, direct answer to every question. Evasiveness creates tension, and usually comes back to haunt you when you try to close.

WHAT THIS TARGET MEANS TO ME: _____

_____
_____

TARGET #6

Target your facts! The best rule is to never tell a lie, or to give information or opinions you can't back up. Promise only what you know you can deliver.

WHAT THIS TARGET MEANS TO ME: _____

_____
_____

14.

The Psychology Of Selling

"If a man can write a better book, preach a better sermon, or make a better mouse-trap, than his neighbor, though he builds his house in the woods, the world will make a beaten path to his door," said Ralph Waldo Emerson.

With all due respects to the wise Emerson, any salesperson who is out there selling in today's competitive marketplace would join me in saying, "It just ain't so!"

If it were so, major companies would not invest millions of dollars on market research, massive advertising, and building strong sales forces. If it were so, door-to-door selling, huge and expensive shopping malls, and premiums would never have come into being. And, if it were so, the millions of salespeople who keep this nation's great private enterprise system moving would be out of jobs.

People don't just buy 99 percent of the products and services in this country; those products and services have to be sold!

WHAT HAPPENS WHEN SOMEONE IS SOLD?

What actually takes place at that magical moment in a sales interview when a prospect becomes a customer?

It's really quite simple: *The prospect makes a decision to buy!* The steps leading up to that decision might be many and complex; that decision might be a product of weeks or even months of work by the salesperson; and that decision might be ever so tenuous; but it's the prospect's decision to buy that makes a sale happen.

So, what's the psychology of selling? Actually, there are many psychological factors at work in the selling process, and the better schooled a salesperson is in all of those factors, the better equipped that salesperson is to move people to act.

It is helpful to understand all the different personality types and how to deal with each, to know the basic motivational factors that cause people to act or not to act, and it is extremely useful to have a working knowledge of how to reduce tension and build trust. Constant reading in those areas can help you to become an increasingly effective salesperson.

MOST SELLING A SIMPLE PROCESS

Selling, in most situations, is really a simple process based on a few principles. Unfortunately, they are easier to understand than they are to remember.

When Vince Lombardi took over the Green Bay Packers football team, he found a defeated, disheartened group of men who were about ready to quit. In the preceding season, they had won only two games. Yet, three years later they won the world championship in professional football, and went on to become what many sportswriters have called "football's greatest dynasty."

What made the difference? Lombardi's message was simple: "We're going to get back to basics and win!" He told those dispirited players, "You're going to learn to run, and block, and tackle. . . . You're going to learn to pass, and kick, and catch the ball!" And, that's exactly what they did.

Every football analyst who studied their phenomenal rise to power came to the same conclusion. The Green Bay Packers won because they became masters at execution. The same players who had lost the year before, and had developed the habit of losing, became almost unbeatable when they mastered the basics.

If your sales have been dragging lately, let me encourage you to study this chapter carefully, and get back to basics so you can win. And, if things have been going well for you, they will go even better if you will stick to the basics.

THE BASICS OF SELLING

It matters little what you are selling, what types of customers you call on, what kind of personality you have, or what kind of economic situation you face; there are certain basic principles that are at work in the buying decision. Understand those basic principles, base all your actions on them, and you can win in enough selling situations to make a very good living.

PRINCIPLE #1: Desire is the key to the buying decision!

It's this simple: When the desire for the product or service you are selling is strong enough to override other desires, the person will buy.

There is a lot of talk in the trade today about "needs-satisfaction selling." The idea is to find a need, or create a need, for the person to buy what you're selling.

Basically, it's a good concept, except that most people in America don't really need what most people are selling. Of course, people need food; but do they really need pre-processed, instant cake mixes in 47 flavors?

Socialist economies and dictatorships focus on the "needs" of the people within their countries. The leaders of the "peoples' government" get together and determine what the people need, and set about to try to make it available.

But the private enterprise system has become the most powerful economic force in the world because it seeks to satisfy the *desires* of people. In a free society, people have the right to choose what they will buy, how much they will buy and, perhaps most important to the salesperson, which of several items they will select and buy.

Frank Bettger, that great salesman of a bygone era, said that the greatest secret he ever learned about selling was, "Show people what they want, and they will move heaven and earth to get it."

DESIRE-SATISFACTION SELLING

For the professional salesperson, desire-satisfaction selling means several important things:

A. *Concentrate your best selling efforts on the people who logically have the greatest desire for what you are selling.*

When the vacuum cleaner was first introduced, department stores refused to carry it because they didn't feel they had the space. "And besides," they argued, "women who can afford carpets can also afford maids to beat their carpets." But the inventor was not to be outdone. He came up with a way to approach his potential customers directly, through salesmen who went into their homes. Within 30 years, those department stores were clamoring for his machines. He had created a market by telling his story to the right people.

B. *Listen to learn the greatest desire you can fulfill.*

Remember, IBM wanted to sell office machines, but their customers wanted to buy information. So, the marketing geniuses of IBM listened to their customers and came up with the concept of "management information systems." Their customers' desires were fulfilled, and IBM has sold a tremendous number of sophisticated and expensive "office machines." Learn to listen for the greatest desire.

C. *Build value by focussing on all the desires your product or service will fulfill.*

The smart real estate salesperson seeks to determine all of the things a prospect wants from a home, carefully searches for the house that most fully meets the desires of the customer, then enthusiastically points out to that customer all the benefits of owning that particular home. When enough value has been built, by satisfying enough desires, the sale is in the bag. This principle holds true for almost any category of product or service.

D. *Effectively balance one set of desires against others that exist.*

Someone described mixed emotions as "watching your mother-in-law drive off a cliff in your new car."

Most customers bring to the selling situation several competing desires. For example, your prospect might want "Tiffany" quality, look, and prestige, but also want a "K-Mart" price. It takes a great deal of skill to make the features and benefits you have to offer override the other desires the prospect may have. But effective salespeople practice until they become masters at it.

BALANCING DESIRE AND NEED

So, where does needs-satisfaction come into the picture?

Many people have difficulty in justifying spending money on something they simply want. They would rather see the desire as a need, then they can justify paying for the item they desire.

"A need gives a customer a reason for doing what he or she wants to do," someone said. For this reason, it is usually more productive to talk to the prospect about needs, rather than desires.

PRINCIPLE #2: Desires can be heightened, or even created.

Love at first sight happens a lot more frequently in movies than it does in selling situations. The skillful salesperson seeks to take the seed of desire that exists, and to intensify it enough to get the person to act immediately.

This is how the salesperson earns his or her commissions. The degree to which a salesperson must be present and actively involved in creating or heightening desire is usually the determining factor in the percentage of the selling price that goes to the salesperson.

Fresh vegetables need only to be attractively displayed in a supermarket to be sold, but to sell a $15,000 automobile, a salesperson must do a lot of heightening of desire.

The single most important way to build desire in the prospect is to sell benefits the prospect will receive from buying and owning that product.

BUILD VALUE THROUGH SELLING BENEFITS

You and your company can decide:

—What your product or service costs to produce.

—How much profit you want to make.

—What similar products and services sell for.

—What price you will charge.

But the customer decides its value! The value of a product or service is the price the customer is willing to pay for it. Thus, when the value to the customer is equal to the price you wish to charge, you've got yourself a sale.

That narrows a salesperson's options down to two. That salesperson can either lower the price, or raise the value to the customer. You can sell it for less, or make it worth more to the customer.

Since most prices are set low enough to be competitive, and in any case can only be lowered to a certain point, the secret in this business of selling is to raise the value of what is to be sold: to lift the price the customer is willing to pay.

It is the salesperson's task to make sure that the prospect is fully aware of all of the benefits he or she will derive from buying and owning what is being sold. That sounds simple enough, but you'd be surprised how many salespeople concentrate mostly on prices, deals, and bargains.

For example, how many times have you shopped for a car and had the salesperson tell you all about the "factory rebate," the "good deal you're being offered," and the fact that "next year's models will cost a lot more." That salesperson is assuming that the car already has enough value to you for you to buy, and that all that is necessary is to convince you that the price is right.

Contrast that with the salesman I described in Chapter Two who asked me if I'd ever owned a Mercedes, and then proceeded to take the next 27 minutes telling and showing me "what's so special about owning a Mercedes." His whole pitch was based on benefits I would receive as an owner of the product he was selling. He concentrated on raising the value of that car to me by selling me benefits.

The amateur relies on statements like: "That's really a good television set," or "Those are on sale this week," or "You really need to go ahead and buy this policy, right now."

But the professional says: "Let me tell you why that is such a great television set. . ." or "We've sold a lot of these at the regular price, and here's why. . ." or "By buying this policy today, you qualify for . . . which means you will be able to. . . ."

When the customer says, "Your price is too high," the amateur says, "I'll talk to the manager and see if I can get you a better deal," but the professional realizes that he or she has not built enough value to make the product or service worth the cost to the customer.

Remember, the single most important way to build desire in prospects is to sell benefits that prospects will receive from buying and owning the product or service!

That leads us to the next basic principle that makes selling a simple process.

PRINCIPLE #3: Personal persuasion is the strongest means of building desire.

Audiovisuals and other sales aids can be very helpful in explaining important features and benefits to prospects, and should be used to maximum advantage.

However, most companies are willing to invest what it takes to keep an effective sales force on the field because they realize the tremendous persuasive power of personal contact.

Remember, the measure of your effectiveness as a salesperson is your power to persuade a substantial number of prospects to purchase your products at the price your company has established.

If desire is the key to the buying decision, the most effective way for the salesperson to persuade with power is to get in touch with all of the desires the customer has—especially the overriding desire—and build all efforts to persuade around those desires. That's why it is so important to ask questions, to listen to the customer, and to observe everything that customer does.

For example, if you are selling power tools and a prospect walks in to buy an electric drill, find out what that customer really wants. Your prospect might be a consumer who only wants a few holes in a wall. That person might not care so much about the drill's reversible motor, the rugged durability of its housing, the convenient controls, or the one-year warranty. What that customer wants is holes in his wall, and he wants to get those holes there as easily and cheaply as possible.

On the other hand, a carpenter who will use that drill every day, sometimes for hours at a time, will have a strong desire for long-lasting durability, plenty of power, ease of operation, and a good warranty.

Always make your appeal to your customer's self-interests. People make buying decisions for their own reasons, not yours!

PRINCIPLE #4: Selling is basically a process of negotiating agreements in which everybody wins.

Whether we are selling a widget for 98 cents, or a building for several million dollars, we are basically negotiating an agreement.

Both the customer and the salesperson bring something of value to the bargaining table. Unless each wants something the other has to offer, there is no selling situation.

Too many salespeople consider price to be the only point for negotiation and spend most of their time, and creative energy, on dealing with that issue. Then they complain that "nobody wants to pay a fair price, anymore," or that their company "charges too much for its products and services."

It is usually quite clear to the customer what desire brings the salesperson to the negotiating table. That salesperson wants the customer's money.

But it is seldom as clear to the salesperson what desires bring the customer into the negotiating situation. Thus, one reason so many sales break down before they really get off the ground is that the salesperson is negotiating with false assumptions. For example, a real estate broker may assume that a client is primarily looking for a comfortable home, at a reasonable price, while the customer is actually much more concerned about making a sound investment or gaining prestige.

The salesperson who understands selling as a negotiating process—from beginning to end—can become a very effective persuader. Here are some tips to help you become a better negotiator:

1. *Do your homework!* Find out as much as you can, in advance, about the prospect you will be attempting to sell.

What makes that person interested in what you are selling? What makes that person hesitant to buy, and buy now? Reliable information, obtained in advance, can help you to know how to approach the prospect.

Also, make sure you know every feature of what you are selling that might in any way be attractive to the prospect.

Prepare well in advance so that every point of your selling proposition will be tailored to the specific needs and desires of that prospect.

Try to find out as much as you can about the actual selling situation you will be facing. For example, a large franchising operation called together a group of potential investors and carefully explained to them their business proposal. It was such a good proposal, and so well presented, that all of the prospects left the meeting excited and ready to get started. Yet, not one of them followed up on the proposition. When the company approached the prospects to find out why they had lost interest, they discovered that while they had explained their proposition well enough for their prospects to understand, they had not explained it well enough for them to be able to explain it to their spouses, their accountants, and their business partners. They had not done enough homework to discover and prepare for other decision-makers who would be involved.

If you would negotiate sales successfully, do your homework!

2. *Seek to understand human nature!* *Why* people do what they do, rather than *what* they do, is often more important for the salesperson to know.

For example, one successful sales manager says that there are basically two kinds of customers: emotional and logical. He instructs his salespeople to sell the emotional people through logic, and the logical people through emotions. The idea is that a person is not going to be outwitted at his or her own game.

Any effort you make toward gaining a better understanding of the motivations people bring to the selling situation will be well worth the time and effort.

3. *Study the negotiating process and techniques!* Many high-pressure salespeople have been greatly dismayed by the Federal Trade Commission's ruling that gave consumers the right to cancel a contract within three days after they had signed it. The action made it harder to intimidate a customer into buying. Such practices have no place in professional selling, anyway.

The real professional salesperson sees selling as a process of negotiating an agreement in which everybody wins. The customer wins because he or she has obtained value for money invested, and the salesperson wins because he or she has obtained money for value given. Moreover, when everybody wins, the customer will tell friends about the pleasure of doing business with the salesperson, and can be expected to help that salesperson make other sales.

I would strongly recommend that any person who wants to become more effective at negotiating sales read *The Art Of Negotiating,* by Gerard I. Nierenberg. The author is a highly skilled and experienced negotiator who explains strategies and tactics that can easily be adapted to the selling situation.

4. *Never allow a customer to become an adversary!* The customer may not always be right, but he's always the customer!

When a customer feels that he or she must lose face to do business with you, it becomes an obstacle over which few people are willing to climb.

Now, I'll grant you that some customers can be real pills. They'll lie to you, cheat you if they can, speak harshly to you, and otherwise make life pretty unpleasant. Some customers act as if you need their "old money" and, unfortunately, they are usually right!

The Chinese have an ancient saying: "He who strikes the first blow admits that his ideas have run out." The amateur says: "I don't have to take this from you, or anybody else!" But the professional sets about to resolve the conflict and restore the good working relationship which creates more sales. If the customer becomes "impossible" to deal with, the professional expends his or her creative energies on cultivating a new customer, rather than on fighting with a disgruntled person.

Being caught in the middle—between an unhappy customer and unyielding people within your company—seems to be one of the hazards of the selling profession. Those people who learn to control their own emotions and successfully negotiate agreements in which everybody wins can write their own tickets to their futures.

The wise salesperson is willing to put aside petty grievances and grudges for the longer-term objective of winning future sales. Even when that salesperson must get tough with a customer, every effort is made to do it in a way that ultimately leads to a resolution of the conflict.

SELLING IS AN ART, NOT A SCIENCE

There are certain basic rules, principles, and guidelines of selling; and to that extent it can be called a science. And, to the extent that selling and psychology are both concerned with human motivations and behavior, it is appropriate to speak of the "psychology of selling."

However, those people who are most successful in selling are those who approach it as an art. They seek to become masters at recognizing and heightening desires, at persuading people to act, at negotiating agreements in which everybody wins, including themselves.

If you would be a successful and professional salesperson, master the basic principles of selling, and practice—using them until you become superb.

* * *

REVIEW AND APPLICATION

What actually takes place at that magical moment in a sales interview when the prospect becomes a customer is that the *prospect makes a decision to buy*. As you review each of the basic principles that underlie that buying decision, list an example from your recent selling experiences and set a strategy for utilizing the principle to increase your effectiveness.

PRINCIPLE #1

Desire is the key to the buying decision!

MY EXAMPLE: _____

MY STRATEGY: _____

PRINCIPLE #2

Desires can be heightened, or even created!

MY EXAMPLE: _____

_____

MY STRATEGY: _____

_____

PRINCIPLE #3

Personal persuasion is the strongest means of building desire!

MY EXAMPLE: _____

_____

MY STRATEGY: _____

_____

PRINCIPLE #4

Selling is basically a process of negotiating agreements in which everybody wins!

MY EXAMPLE: _____

_____

MY STRATEGY: _____

_____

15.

You Can Become A Master Closer

The best presentation in the world is of little value unless it results in a sale! If you would become a *professional* salesperson, you must become a *master closer*; you must master the art of effective closing.

As a professional sales trainer, I have an opportunity to meet, observe, and train thousands of salespeople every year. I talk to those people, I *listen* to those people, and I study what they do.

In all my years of studying why successful people are successful, and why unsuccessful people fail, there are four things I have never seen:

First, I have never seen a successful salesperson who could not close effectively. Sure, I've seen some order-takers who were always taking advantage of other people's closing expertise, but their careers were usually short-lived.

Secondly, I have never seen an effective closer who was not successful, if that person was willing to work.

Thirdly, I have never seen an effective closer who could not improve his or her closing techniques. Closing is an art—not a science—and there is always a better way to do it.

And last, I have never seen an effective closer who was not looking for ways to become more effective at closing.

WHAT IS A MASTER CLOSER?

Master closers are not all that easy to find. In most sales organizations, less than 10 percent of the sales force can be classified as effective closers. It is not at all uncommon to find only one or two master closers in a company with more than a hundred salespeople.

So, how do you spot the master closers? They have six characteristics that always set them apart from the order-takers.

1. The first thing you will notice about a master closer is that he or she has a *strong desire to close.* You look for a person who likes to win, a person who enjoys getting people to do things, a person who thrives on making a sale. Some sales managers call it a "killer instinct." Part of the motivation may be to make a lot of money, but it usually runs deeper than that. The master closer usually savours the moment of victory, especially when the sale is difficult to make.

2. The second thing you can spot about a master closer is *confidence!* Look for self-confidence, the feeling that the person is capable of meeting the challenge, no matter how great it is. Look for confidence in one's company—a strong belief that he or she works for a good organization that can be trusted by their customers. And, look for enthusiasm born of confidence in the product or service. The master closer ex-

udes self-confidence, confidence in the company he or she represents, and assurance that all the benefits promised will come to the customer who buys the products and services.

3. Always look for a person who is *alert: one who is aware of everything!* The master closer watches the prospect and is sensitive to any tension present, aware of the strength or weakness of the trust bond, on guard for any change in mood, or the faintest signal that the person is ready to buy. That master closer paces every step of the close with the precision of timing that will remind you of a symphony conductor.

4. The master closer *believes in the process.* Qualifying prospects, for the master closer, is not a matter of looking at a person's clothes, or environment, or other superficial signs. They move in for the close, give the customer every opportunity to buy, and trust that customer to make his or her own decision. They don't make judgments on who can or will buy, based on shallow information. They believe in the selling process and in the ability of the client to choose, not in their own abilities to choose for their clients.

5. *Skill in using closing techniques* is another sign of a master closer. They have studied the techniques of very successful salespeople and adapted them to their own styles and selling situations. They have practiced those techniques until they can use them in their sleep. They have developed a knack for knowing which closing technique will work best with their own personalities, with the personalities of their clients, and in particular selling situations. They might even use several different closing techniques on one prospect. Master closers are like master painters; they always select the most effective tool to get the precise effect they are aiming for.

6. And finally, you can usually spot the master closers *out front!* They are usually leading the pack, or well on their way to leading the pack. They are competitive, always open to learn, always readjusting their goals upward, and reaching out for new challenges. They always aim high because they

have developed the attitude of success, and will not settle for less than they can be.

Master closers make sales, but order-takers make excuses. Ask order-takers why they did not close a sale and you'll be amazed at some of the excuses you'll hear.

They sometimes remind me of the people who were asked by an insurance company to explain how their automobile accidents occurred. One guy said, "I took one look at my mother-in-law and went right off the road." Another fellow said, "The pedestrian hit my car, and went right under it!" A lady explained, "The other car was weaving all over the road and I had to swerve several times before I hit it." Those people did not intend to be funny, but they were! And, the order-takers sometimes sound just as funny as they try to explain away their failures.

If order-takers would put half as much creativity into developing their closing skills as they do into their excuses, they could close 10 times as many sales. If they invested one-tenth the energy in closing sales as they do in carrying around those feelings of defeat and failure, they could watch their closing averages take off like a rocket.

WHAT ARE YOU WILLING TO INVEST?

A young woman went to work for a major fashion house and, because the company thought she had bright prospects, they assigned her to work with and study the most successful salesperson on their force. The first day out, the trainee went to her role model's hotel room at 7:00 am. As she knocked on the door she heard a voice. "I hope I'm not interrupting," she said. "Oh, no!" her leader replied, "I'm just practicing my closes." After a vigorous day of work and a leisurely dinner, they each returned to their rooms.

While studying some sales literature, the trainee came across something she didn't understand so she went to her leader's room. Again—although it was now 9:00 pm—she found the sales leader practicing her closes. "Do you do that every day?" she asked.

"Every day," said the very successful saleswoman, "including Sundays . . . If I don't practice every single day, I lose my edge."

"How long have you been selling for this company?" the young woman asked, and the old pro said, "For 30 years."

People say to me, "I want to become an effective closer." I always ask them, "What are you willing to invest?"

Are you willing to read every book and article, and listen to every single cassette that might have something to teach you about closing? Are you willing to study the outstanding closers you know and see how they do it? Are you willing to spend hours and hours practicing the closing techniques you learn?

When people say to me, "I'm closing more sales now than I closed last year!" I say to them, "Good! But are you closing all that you could close?" When people say to me, "I wish I could close like you do!" I say to them, "If you will invest one-tenth the time and effort that I have invested in learning how to close effectively, you can also close 10 times more effectively."

In the next chapter I am going to give you 12 of the most successful closing techniques ever developed by the top professionals. Using these techniques, you can become a master closer—*provided* that you are willing to invest enough of yourself in learning, practicing, and using them.

But first, I must tell you something that may shock you! The average salesperson uses less than 10 percent of what he or she knows about closing sales. What you know about closing sales is important, but what you do with what you know is what really counts.

Right now, let's concentrate on reinforcing some basics we all know but tend to forget about closing.

1. *Ask for the order!* People don't *buy,* they are *sold!* The most common reason that salespeople walk out without an order is that they fail to ask the customer to buy. We can't wait for the customer to say, "I'll buy it." We must close the sale!

2. *People only buy when they understand the product or service and what it will do for them.* It is frustrating to our prospects and a waste of our time to try to close before the customers clearly understand what we are selling and what we are asking them to do.

3. *There is almost always one key issue that must be settled in the prospect's mind before that prospect will buy.* It might be a fear, or a concern, or a grudge against our company or product, but whatever it is, that key issue must be settled before we can close the sale.

4. *There is almost always an overriding desire, problem, or need that makes the product or service attractive to the prospect.* What matters most is not what we like best about what we are selling but what the customer likes most. When we help people discover what they want, and then help them discover how to get it through our products and services, it is easy to close by targeting the benefit that they want. As salespeople, we are not there to *change* our customers' minds about what they want; we are there to give them what they want to buy.

5. *People have trouble making big decisions so most successful closers give them an opportunity to make many little decisions.* A prospect might not be willing to commit to a

$2,000 life insurance premium, so the smart closer asks him to decide who will be his beneficiary. Here's an easy way to remember that very important principle.

Do you know what a "monkeyfist" is? A large ship has to be tied up to a pier with a huge rope that weighs several hundred pounds. There's no way a sailor could throw that big rope over to someone on the pier. So he throws over a smaller rope, with one end tied to the large rope, or hauser. The guy on the pier uses that to pull over the big, heavy rope. Now to make that process easy, they attach a small ball, which they call a *"monkeyfist,"* to the other end of that little rope. This makes it easy to throw, and easy for the guy on the pier to catch.

The next time you find a customer balking at a big decision, back up and throw him a "monkeyfist." This is what some people call a trial close; but whatever you call it, it helps close sales. Our goal in closing a sale is to make it as easy as possible for the customer to say that big word, "Yes!" And, 10 small "yesses" beat one big "No!"

6. *Try one more time!* When all else has failed, and it appears that the final word is "No," try to close one more time. If tactfully done, it costs nothing but a little time. And, if it only works one out of 10 times, you can boost your closing average by 10 percent. That's a darn good return on investment.

DO YOU WANT TO BE A MASTER CLOSER?

Do you want to be a master closer? What are you willing to invest?

Some people will tell you that master closers are born that way, but the professional salespeople who have mastered the art will tell you in a minute that they are *made*. And they will agree that anyone can become an effective closer if that person is willing to invest what it takes.

REMINDERS

The average salesperson uses less than 10% of what he or she knows about closing sales. In this chapter we sought to remind you of some often overlooked basics about closing—facts we all know, but tend to forget. As you review, think about a sale you made (or lost) as a result of remembering (or failing to remember) each basic.

BASIC #1

Ask for the order! People don't buy—they are sold! The most common reason salespeople walk out without an order is they fail to ask the customer to buy.

I SAW THIS FACT, WHEN: _____

_____

_____

BASIC #2

People only buy when they understand the product or service and what it will do for them. It is frustrating to customers to try to close a sale before that customer understands the product, and what we are asking them to do.

I SAW THIS FACT, WHEN: _____

_____

_____

BASIC #3

There is almost always one key issue in the prospect's mind that must be settled before the sale can be closed. It might be a fear, a grudge, a concern—or whatever—but it must be settled in the customer's mind before he or she will buy.

I SAW THIS FACT, WHEN: _____

_____

_____

BASIC #4

There is almost always one overriding desire, or need, or problem that makes the product attractive to the customer. As salespeople, we are not there to change our customers' minds, we are there to give them what they want to buy.

I SAW THIS FACT, WHEN: _____

_____

_____

BASIC #5

People often have trouble making big decisions. Closing sales is easier when we give people an opportunity to make many little decisions. Ten small "yesses" beat one big "no" every time!

I SAW THIS FACT, WHEN: _____

_____

_____

BASIC #6

Persistence pays off! When all else has failed, and it appears that the final word is "No," try one more close. If it only works one time out of 10, you can boost your closing average by 10 percent.

I SAW THIS FACT, WHEN: _____

_____
_____

16.

Professional Closing Techniques

Closing sales is an art—not a science! That means that professional salespeople are artists instead of scientists. What's the difference?

The person engaged in research leaves what is known and proven, and constantly reaches out for the unknown. Scientists are always trying to discover why things are the way they are, and they are always testing what others have found effective, in their efforts to find a new way. They have a valuable place!

But professional salespeople are more like the artist. They accept what has been learned and seek to make it work for themselves. They are not trying to prove that their theories are right, only to use tested and proven methods to achieve their goals—to close sales. Professional salespeople are not so concerned with why a certain close works, as they are with finding the most effective close for a particular situation. They are not always trying to rewrite the book on effective closing techniques. What they try to do is to use those tested and proven methods of closing to maximum advantage.

But this is a scientific age, an age where science is held in high regard. People want to be known as innovators. That's fine for the scientist who gets paid to experiment, to test out theories, to make great discoveries.

That scientist might make 10,000 experiments before finding a method that will work. However, a salesperson, on straight commission, would starve to death making 10,000 pitches without closing a sale.

Salespeople don't get paid to experiment; they don't get paid to make new discoveries; they don't get paid to prove their theories are right.

Professional salespeople know that they get paid to do one thing—sell! And, especially when it comes to closing, they stick with what has been proven to be effective.

That's why they often close as many as 30 or 40—sometimes even 50 percent of their sales. They stick with what they know will work. At first, they stick with them because other professionals have shown that they will work. Later they stick with proven techniques because they know those tested methods will work for them.

It is only when the professional salesperson has mastered the basics and builds up an impressive track record in selling that he or she will test a new theory.

12 PROVEN CLOSING TECHNIQUES

The closing techniques I'm going to share with you are *proven winners*—methods of closing sales that really work.

Professional Closing Techniques 187

No one of these closes will work on every customer, and some of them might not fit your personality, or what you are selling. The more familiar you are with all of them, the more easily you will be able to find just the right close, for *every* customer, and for *every* selling situation.

Here they are—an even dozen closing techniques—all tested and proven by some of the top salespeople during the last hundred years.

CLOSING TECHNIQUE #1: The "Constant Close Approach"

The idea is to make every statement or question a *trial* close, including the opening sentence. The earliest sales training program of Sears, Roebuck and Company emphasized the power of this approach. Their trainers would say to new salespeople, "Never ask a customer, 'Can I help you?' but ask a question that affirms that the person is there to buy something."

Whether or not the constant close technique will work in your line of selling, most of us could learn something valuable from the idea behind it. "Can I help you?" is a dumb question. It's like saying, "If you are looking for the Salvation Army, you've come to the right place." Our customers are not there to look for help, they are there to help *us!* "Do you have a particular style in mind?" recognizes that the customer will buy, if he or she finds just the right item.

Constant closers use a lot of questions like, "Isn't that right, Mr. Smith?" or, "Don't you agree that this service will solve that problem, Mrs. Smith?" Constant closes are offensive to some customers; use them carefully!

CLOSING TECHNIQUE #2: The "Summary Close"

The salesperson recaps all of the features and benefits, asking for the customer's agreement on each point. This technique can be used effectively as a partial close in almost any selling situation, or it can be used effectively as a sole closing technique. A temptation with the summary close is to emphasize every point of the presentation with equal weight or to run over the presentation again. The summary points that should get the most attention are those that seem to be most important to the client!

CLOSING TECHNIQUE #3: The "Alternate Close"

In the alternate close, you allow the customer to say "yes" by stating a preference. "Would you like this delivered Tuesday, or would Wednesday be better?" Here, the idea is to allow the customer to make a choice on the terms of the sale, rather than making that choice on whether or not to buy.

Alternate closes work well with people who are definitely considering buying, but have a little difficulty making up their minds. Caution! Alternate closes can backfire with customers who are highly independent or suspicious. Make sure the trust bond is strong before you try an alternate close—but it can be a very valuable closing tool.

CLOSING TECHNIQUE #4: The "Assume the Sale Close"

In using the assumed sale close, you take it for granted that the customer is going to buy. If you are pretty sure that the customer is ready to buy, you might say, "How soon must you have this?" Again, this only works when the trust bond is strong and you have seen some pretty strong buying signals. Some salespeople, with very assertive personalities, use this approach all the time—and use it very effectively. They pop the question and then don't say another word until the customer answers. The theory is that whoever speaks first after the question has been asked, *loses!* It's a strong closing technique, but it works well with many customers.

CLOSING TECHNIQUE #5: The "Little Decision Close"

When you sense that a customer is the type that has trouble making big decisions, you offer them opportunities to make many little decisions. The idea is that once the affirmative decision ball starts rolling, most people will just follow the momentum, and ultimately sign the order. This is one of the most widely used techniques, because it works well with so many people! Most people have trouble making up their minds, and look to a salesperson to make up their minds for them.

Again, watch out for the independent type of person who wants to make a big decision first. Professional buyers often pride themselves on resisting those little questions, and may even make a game out of leading a salesperson into a trap. They will say a dozen *yesses,* and then one big *no!* The key to the little decision close is to know your customer; observe every change in mood; constantly check the trust bond you have built up.

CLOSING TECHNIQUE #6: The "Start Wrapping It Up Close!"

Do something which the customer will have to stop you from doing to avoid giving consent. This "do something" approach to closing assumes the sale and sets in motion a physical action which must be overtly stopped to avoid saying yes. It's based on the theory of the old carnival barker, who always had professional pushers in the audience. The paid pushers would start at the back of the crowd as the barker made his spiel, and gently start the crowd moving closer to the door. Once a person was physically moved close to the door, it took a lot of self-confidence for him to stop, turn around and face the crowd, and walk out—so most of them would go in.

This closing technique is dynamite! When you start the ball rolling by a physical action, like filling out an order blank, the prospect must take strong action to stop you. Your self-confidence is the key to making it work. But be very careful where, and on whom you use it. It can explode in your face.

CLOSING TECHNIQUE #7: The "Better Act Now Close!"

Focus on changing conditions that make it wise for the person to act immediately on your proposal. It sounds like a high-pressure tactic, but it can be very useful with the customer who always wants to put off a decision. "Our production is almost sold up on this item . . . I can give you a definite delivery date today, but you may have to wait a long time if you postpone a decision." That's a strong reason to buy now! Make sure that the coming event you predict is believable to the client. If you predict that prices will rise, be sure the client agrees it's a good possibility.

CLOSING TECHNIQUE #8: The "Bring Your Own Witness Tactic"

Giving the client names of people who have already bought and are satisfied customers is often a strong closing tool. This is particularly true of people who buy on the motivation of imitation. Most people are influenced by the decisions of other people they respect. Some successful salespeople will ask satisfied customers if they will give a letter telling briefly how satisfied they are with a product, company, and service. A few even go so far as to call a satisfied customer from the prospect's phone, and ask that customer to tell the new prospect how satisfied he or she is. This closing technique works very well with people who are strongly motivated by the *herd instinct*. *Caution:* If your customer is a strong individualist, to talk about all the satisfied customers you have might cause that person to say, "If everybody else is doing it, why should I?" Also, be careful that you don't allow the prospect to use "checking with some of those people you mentioned" as a *stalling* tactic.

One indication of how strong a selling tool this is: it is so widely used in television commercials. Celebrity endorsements influence many, many people to buy.

CLOSING TECHNIQUE #9: The "Premium Offer Tactic"

When a customer has almost decided to buy, but wants to wait, you pull out a "bargain for acting now." The strength of this approach lies in the fact that most people want to get something for nothing. The key here is, don't spill the beans too early! And, always offer a premium that has value to your prospect. An 8"x10" color photo of your *dog* won't get it! A realistic incentive—not something you claim to be 10 times as valuable as the product you sell—can very often move a hesitant prospect to buy now.

CLOSING TECHNIQUE #10: The "Close on Every Objection Tactic"

Many very successful closers take every objection as a buying signal. Once they have satisfactorily dealt with the objection, they ask for the order.

Closing on every objection can be a very strong technique for closing the sale, or it can be used effectively as a pre-close trial technique to test the water and see how close you are to a sale.

CLOSING TECHNIQUE #11: The "Let the Customer Fill Out the Order Tactic"

This works well with an application blank which doubles as an order blank. You might say, "Would you write your name right here exactly as you would like it to appear on the title?" Or, "I'd like you to give me the following information, please." The power of this tactic is that it gives the prospect something to do without actually spending money. Once the customer starts writing, shifting the document from "application blank" to "order blank" is usually relatively easy.

CLOSING TECHNIQUE #12: "Ask for the Order"

Of course you should always ask in one way or another for the customer to buy, but this technique compels you to simply *ask* for the sale. "Shall I wrap it up for you?" Under certain conditions, this can be very effective. Notice that I did not say "beg for the order." The reason for asking for the order must always be based on the customer's desire to buy—not your desire to make a sale.

So, there they are: a whole dozen closing techniques developed by the pros, used successfully by many of the top salespeople around the world, and proven to be effective! Master them, and you can close a lot of sales you might now be missing.

* * *

REVIEWING CLOSING TECHNIQUES

Here are the 12 tested and proven closing techniques. We suggest you draw a circle around those you have not yet used, and try to use one the next time you are in an appropriate situation.

TECHNIQUE #1

The constant close. Here, the idea is to make every statement and question a trial close.

TECHNIQUE #2

The summary close. Recap all of the features and benefits, asking the customer to agree on each point. Note: This technique can be used in conjunction with most other closes.

TECHNIQUE #3

The alternate close. "Do you want it in black, or do you prefer red?" "Shall we deliver it Wednesday, or would Friday be better for you?" This helps the indecisive customer select, rather than forcing a decision on whether to buy, or not to buy.

TECHNIQUE #4

Assume the sale. You take it for granted that the customer is going to buy now. You might say, "How soon must you have this?" It is important, when using this technique, to say nothing after you have asked the question. Whoever speaks first, loses.

TECHNIQUE #5

The little decision close. Allow the customer to make all of the little decisions about the sale. Once you have enough little "yesses," write up the order.

TECHNIQUE #6

Start wrapping it up. Do something the customer will have to stop you from doing to avoid giving consent. The strength of this technique is that it sets in motion a physical action that must be overtly stopped to avert the sale. It's a strong closing technique.

TECHNIQUE #7

The better act now close. Focus on changing conditions that make it wise for the customer to act now, as opposed to waiting. Make sure that the "coming event" you predict is believable to the client.

TECHNIQUE #8

The bring your own witness tactic. People often buy to imitate others they admire and respect. Show letters of testimony from satisfied customers, use lists of people who have bought, and invite your prospect to get on the bandwagon.

TECHNIQUE #9

The premium offer tactic. When the customer wants to buy, but hesitates to act, pull out a "bargain for acting now." The key here is not to "spill the beans too early." Wait until all issues are settled, except the issue of when to buy, then introduce the "something for nothing" incentive.

TECHNIQUE #10

The close on every objection tactic. Many successful salespeople take every objection as a buying signal. Once they have satisfactorily dealt with the objection, they ask for the order. This can also be used effectively as a trial close technique.

TECHNIQUE #11

The let the customer fill out the order tactic. The key to successful use of this approach is to ask the customer for information on a form that will later be used as an order blank. Some salespeople feel that, once the prospect starts writing, the sale is in the bag.

TECHNIQUE #12

The ask for the order tactic. Of course, you always ask for the order in one way or another. But in using this tactic, you simply ask the customer to buy with a question like, "Shall I wrap it up for you?" Note: Never beg for an order! The customer buys for his reason—not yours!

17.

Turn Objections Into Sales

Objections are to the salesperson what symptoms are to the medical doctor. They point to a problem that must be dealt with.

The doctor diagnoses what is wrong with a patient by the symptoms that are described by the patient, and the symptoms that can be observed through listening, looking, and testing. When the patient says, "I have a headache," or a fever is detected, the doctor sets about to analyze what causes the pain or the high temperature.

Likewise, the professional salesperson looks on objections as indications that there is a concern, or a problem, that must be resolved before the sale can be completed.

In fact, objections are the salesperson's most valuable source of feedback. They enable you to keep check on the tension level, on the trust bond you have established, on the key issue to be resolved, on the priorities and desires of your customer, on everything you need to monitor during the sales interview.

"I always welcome—even encourage—objections," one highly successful saleswoman told me recently. "The hardest person in the world to sell is the customer who sits there like a bump on a log during the whole presentation, then says, 'You have a nice product, and I like your company, but I'm not interested.' When that person ushers you to the door, you know you've struck out completely," she continued.

"In fact," she added, "if the customer does not object to something, I usually try to force an objection to get them involved . . . 'That's nice' is the worst thing a customer can say to me."

The amateur takes the opposite approach. When a customer objects, the amateur raises the volume level, increases the speed of the words, and tries to beat down the objection. That's not selling; it's manipulation, or an attempt at coercion.

POINTERS FOR HANDLING OBJECTIONS

Just as closing sales has definite and proven approaches, so does handling objections. What follows are some pointers on handling objections, pointers that have proven to be successful in turning objections into sales.

POINTER #1: Be prepared!

Know in advance what objections are likely to arise and be prepared to deal effectively with them.

Often, if you know what objections your customer will raise, you can head them off before they are raised. You might say something like, "Many of my customers are concerned about high interest rates, and I imagine that concerns you, too." By bringing the issue up yourself, you let the prospect know that you are not afraid to deal with it. Then, you can come back with, "I've got some great news for you! We've solved that problem, and here's how...."

When a customer does raise an objection, you know how to handle it *if you have adequately prepared*. Many successful salespeople use the "If the customer says" technique. They write down and memorize an answer to any objection the customer might raise. Usually, they will slightly paraphrase their answer, so it won't come out canned, or rehearsed. And, they always tailor it to the specific customer. But just knowing in advance what you will say can be a big help in answering objections confidently. And, a confident answer is always best!

POINTER #2: Avoid creating unnecessary objections!

How do salespeople create unnecessary objections? Here are a few of the more common ways:

1. Salespeople sometimes fail to make sure the customer understands the product or service, fail to make the proposition clear, or fail to communicate exactly what they want the customer to do. If the customer does not understand, you can be sure that customer will object. It's not a matter of explaining everything so clearly that a dummy could understand it, it's a matter of making sure *the customer understands it!*

2. Another way salespeople create unnecessary objections is by missing buying signals until the customer changes his or her mind. Some salespeople get so caught up in what they are doing that they miss what the customer is doing, and talk themselves right out of an easy sale. Watch for any buying signal, and take advantage of it.

3. Salespeople often create needless objections by failing to suggest an easy action for the customer to take. Don't wait for the customer to make up his own mind; he may never do it! Many customers want a salesperson to make up their minds for them. Be nice, accommodate them! It will make both of you happy!

4. Sometimes hungry, or timid salespeople *beg* for an order until the customer objects. *Never beg for an order!* Customers buy for *their* reasons—not *yours!*

POINTER #3: Pin down the real objection!

The most important step in handling objections is to understand those objections. Some prospects become masters at throwing up a smokescreen! They'll give you five reasons why they don't want to buy today, but when you look carefully, they all mean the same thing.

Remember J.P. Morgan's famous explanation of why people do things? He said, there are always two reasons people have for doing everything: "The reason they *give*, and the *real* reason."

Defining a person's real objection is often the toughest part of closing the sale. Those real reasons are often so well hidden that it takes real perception to zero-in on just what the person is hiding.

For example, a customer might say, "We are very happy with our present supplier." The real objection might be that he hates your company's credit manager, or feels miffed because of something someone in your territory did to him when he was a trainee. Until that real objection is pinpointed, you are wasting your time to talk about the much better service you can give than the present supplier, the superiority of your products or services, or any other points you might bring up.

How To Detect a Smokescreen

How do you know when an objection is real, and when it is just a smokescreen to cover up a deeper objection? There are several symptoms that can be revealed by asking yourself several questions.

First, when in the interview did the objection come up? If a prospect greets you at the door and says, "I don't need anything your company makes," that might mean one thing. If you've shown that customer the complete line and you still get the same objection, you've got a different problem. "I don't need anything," stated early as an objection, is often a standard ploy a busy person uses to dismiss salespeople. If the prospect listens to your entire presentation, and shows interest by asking questions, then says, "I don't need anything," you can bet your bottom dollar there is a deeper reason.

Second, what mood is conveyed by the prospect's expression, tone of voice, and physical actions? If the customer gets up, walks toward the door, hands you your coat and says, "See me in six months!" that might say, "I'm not sufficiently sold to act now." But if the prospect says, "Gee, I don't know . . . I might be in a better position to talk with you six months from now," it probably means, "Give me one good solid reason why I should buy today."

Third, you might ask yourself, how many objections has this prospect thrown my way? Or, how many different ways has this person said the same thing? If the prospect shows interest, but keeps throwing up smokescreens and coming back to the same objection, chances are pretty good you don't yet know the real objection.

How do you pinpoint the real objection? When you get the feeling you are suffocating in all of the smoke, you might try one of these ploys.

TACTICS FOR PINPOINTING THE REAL OBJECTION

1. Ask for a "what-if" commitment. When a customer keeps coming back to price, for example, you might ask, "If I could show you how this product could save you much more than it costs, would you buy it today?" If that prospect answers "yes," you've found the real issue that must be settled. If the prospect hedges with something like, "I'm not sure," you're probably chasing a smokescreen. Clear up the smokescreen, and the price problem will disappear.

2. Try a summary close, testing carefully the customer's reaction to each feature and benefit. You might find that the prospect is not really sold on one of the features you have presented and is using price as the smokescreen to cover up that fact.

3. Sometimes it works best to just come out and ask, "Why?" If the prospect says, "I'm just not ready to buy," after showing a real interest, ask "Why?" You might find that the customer is not yet convinced that what you are selling will do all that you promise.

Whatever tactic you use, target the real issue! Get the real objection fixed clearly in your own mind, and make sure you understand the problem. Then, focus the real issue with the client! Once the real objection is out on the table, the tension is usually relieved, and that objection can be dealt with effectively.

Research has shown that failure to understand the problem is the number one reason salespeople fail to handle objections properly! Learn to pinpoint the real objection, and half of the battle is already won!

POINTER #4: Deal effectively with the four most common reasons people don't buy!

Turn Objections Into Sales

The number one reason people don't buy is *"no confidence."* They have no confidence in the person making the presentation, or no confidence in the product or service, or no confidence in the company.

A no confidence vote, in the form of an objection, is usually very hard to pin down, and sometimes even harder to fix. But, almost always, it must be fixed before a sale can be made! Usually, when the lack of confidence is directed toward the company, it is best to bring in management on the solution.

Where the product or service is involved, it usually centers on the fact that the customer does not believe that what is offered will meet his or her needs. One way to deal with that objection is to stage a trial demonstration. Another is to get a minimal order to be used on a trial basis by the customer. Sometimes, confidence can be built through testimonials by satisfied users in similar situations.

Whatever the tactic, persistence provides the best chance of winning out in the end.

The number two most common reason people don't buy is *"no need."*

When a customer objects that there is no need for the product or service, what that customer is usually saying is that the desire to buy has not been sufficiently stimulated. Very few prospects really *need* what most of us are selling, anyway! They buy it because they *want* it!

When a prospect says he or she has no need for the product or service, go back to asking questions to try to uncover that desire you have not yet found. Remember, once you help someone discover what they want, they will move heaven and earth to get it.

The third most common reason people fail to buy is that they have *"no money."* Sometimes it is stated that the price is too high. As with the "no need" objection, this one usually means the person is not willing to pay the price because the desire has not yet been uncovered. Uncover the desire, and you've got yourself a sale.

If the person appears interested, but balks at the price, concentrate on building value. Keep pulling out new benefits for the customer and reminding the customer of benefits he or she particularly liked. When that prospect is convinced that the value is too great to pass up, you can close the sale!

And the fourth most common objection customers offer is, *"no hurry."* They want someone else to be in on the decision, they want to wait a while, or they want to look around some more!

To deal effectively witn the delay objection, one question must be settled right away—does the prospect have the authority to give you the order? If not, start immediately to try to get to the one who *can* make the decision. If the prospect says, "I'll talk to them about it," try every way possible to see the decision-maker yourself! Otherwise, you can write off the sale nine times out of ten.

If the person can buy, try these tactics. Give *immediacy* to their action, as with the "coming event" close we discussed. Build value, value, and more value. Try to establish psychological ownership, through a trial ownership, a demonstrator model, or some other approach. Sometimes you can overcome the objection with a "sweetener" like a price break, or a premium. If all else fails, make a definite date to follow up!

Most objections raised will fall into one of these four categories—no confidence, no desire or need, price too high or no money, and no hurry.

Whatever the objection stated, you must first isolate the **real** objection and target your solution to *that!* Objections don't frighten the professional salesperson, but they do give valuable clues to determine what's wrong; then fix it!

POINTER #5: Review your handling of objections after each sales interview and prepare to do a better job of handling those objections when they arise again!

John D. Rockefeller once told a reporter that much of his success came from his practice of giving himself a daily check-up. For 10 minutes, just before he dropped off to sleep at night, he would review his actions during the day, he said. He tried to determine why certain of his actions were successful, and why certain actions failed. Using this nightly check-up, Mr. Rockefeller would seek to constantly refine and improve his actions.

That's a great idea! But, let me suggest that you take it one step further and ask yourself after each call—"How well did I handle my prospect's objections?" Try to remember each objection raised and analyze the way you handled it. You might make some interesting discoveries. When you are in the midst of giving a presentation or a sales pitch, you may not be able to recognize the hidden meanings of objections. But as you think over those objections afterwards, you can sort out exactly *why* they came up, *what* they meant, and *how effectively* you handled each.

As you practice this, you will become so attuned to it that you will be able to do it during sales interviews as *each* objection comes up.

TURN OBJECTIONS INTO SALES

Amateurs ignore, or are intimidated by, objections, but professional salespeople use them as a feedback mechanism to determine what is going wrong, and fix it!

An objection may be a buying signal, a request for more information, a statement of a key issue that must be settled, or a combination of all those things. Successful salespeople learn how to use objections as a doctor uses symptoms: to diagnose what needs to be dealt with.

Your sensitivity in observing objections, and your skill in handling them effectively, can be very valuable tools in your sales career.

* * *

REVIEW AND APPLICATION

We will review each of the five pointers for handling objections and give you a question that will help you think through how you can effectively utilize each one:

POINTER #1

Be prepared! Know in advance what objections are likely to come up and exactly how you will handle each one.

HOW DO YOU:

1. Seek to handle objections before they arise?

_____

_____

2. Prepare yourself to answer any objection the customer might raise? _____

_____

_____

POINTER #2

Avoid creating unnecessary objections. Some objections arise because the salesperson fails to make sure the customer understands the product, service or proposition, or misses buying signals, or fails to suggest simple solutions.

HOW DO YOU:

1. Avoid creating unnecessary objections? _____

_____
_____

2. Know when you have created an objection?

_____
_____
_____

POINTER #3

Understand the objection! The stated objection is often not the real objection. Before you can successfully deal with an objection, you must understand what it is, and what it means.

HOW DO YOU:

1. Separate real objections from "smokescreens"?

_____
_____
_____

2. Determine what the objection really means?

_____
_____
_____

POINTER #4

Deal effectively with the four most common reasons people don't buy. People don't buy because of: no confidence, no perceived need, no money (not enough value), and no hurry.

HOW DO YOU:

2. Handle the problem of "no confidence" in you, your company, or product? _____

_____

_____

2. Deal with the person who feels "no need" for what you are selling? _____

_____

_____

3. Solve the "no money" problem? _____

_____

_____

4. Handle the person who is in "no hurry" to buy?

_____

_____

_____

POINTER #5

Review your handling of objections after each sales interview and prepare to do a better job of handling those objections when they arise again!

What three objections arise most often in your sales interviews and how do you handle each:

1. Objection: _____
   Strategy: _____

2. Objection: _____
   Strategy: _____

3. Objection: _____
   Strategy: _____

18.

How To Turn Stalls Into Action

How do you spell *frustration?* Most salespeople spell it S-T-A-L-L.

The customer says, "I like your product; I will probably buy it . . . but I'm going to wait awhile!"

Or maybe it comes out like this: "Your product is okay, and we've always enjoyed doing business with your company . . . but your price is too high!"

Aside from popping a pill to ease your tension and heartburn, what can you do? Do you play it like the amateurs who walk out patting themselves on the back for making a good presentation? Do you wait for that customer to call you?

If you do either one of those things, chances are pretty good that a competitor will soon come in and walk away with the sale you made! Professional salespeople are too darned busy to waste time selling their products and services *for their competitors!*

When a customer stalls, or puts off a buying decision, the pros consider it a challenge to do combat! They know that a sale is not a sale until they get an order, that a sale *almost* made is worth fighting for, and the pros know it will probably never be easier to close a sale than *now!*

They go into action! But what do they *do?*

FOCUS THE ISSUE

The first thing they do is try to pin down exactly what the stall means! They start asking questions! They try to get into the customer's head and find out what's really going on! They try to see things from the customer's point of view!

Professionals know that you cannot fight an enemy if you can't find that enemy. Like a doctor, they can't treat an illness until they discover exactly what the illness is, and what is causing it.

The pros are too wise to try to fight a smokescreen with another smokescreen! So they set about to ask questions to determine exactly what they are dealing with.

Is the customer's stall on price a ploy to buy time to get a competitor's bid? If so, who is the competitor? Or, is it a tactic to try to bargain for a better price? Maybe that customer has already seen several bids that are lower than yours. Maybe the customer wants your product or service, but can't justify paying more money than a competitor charges for a similar service.

Or, is the problem something that has to do with the customer's situation? If it's a retailer, are inventories too high? Is the customer waiting for an improvement in the economy?

It could be something even more elusive: maybe the customer is trying to punish your company for some perceived mistreatment. Maybe, the stall is the standard tactic the customer uses with all salespeople to say "no" tactfully. The customer won't say "no," just, "We'll call you!"

Remember, you can't fight a smokescreen with a smokescreen! The nature of the issue of concern determines the tactic you will use to counter it. Find out the real issue, and you might be able to close the sale by satisfactorily dealing with that issue. Keep pressing for a decision, without knowing the issue to be settled and, at best, you are wasting time. At worst, you might do irreparable harm to your relationship with that client.

TACTICS THAT WORK

So, how do you find the key issue? Here are several tactics used by some of the top salespeople in the country.

TACTIC #1: Isolate the reason for the stall by a "what if" question!

"If we could settle the question of price, would you order today?" Or, "If I could make this offer attractive enough today, can we do business?" You ask a question that seeks to determine if the stated issue is the real issue. The two keys to using this tactic are: be very specific in your question, and keep absolutely quiet after you ask the question. Be careful not to promise a lower price, or throw in a "sweetener" unless you are prepared to back it up! You are only offering to settle the price question!

If the prospect agrees that a deal is possible immediately once the price problem is settled, you move in to settle the price problem. If the prospect says there is no deal, even if the price question is settled, you know that you are fighting a smokescreen, so you keep probing!

TACTIC #2: Play a hunch!

If you have reason to suspect that a competitor is involved, ask! "Have you been quoted a lower price?" Or, "Are you planning to get bids on this project?"

Of course, you don't want to give the customer any ideas about who can give lower prices, so don't use this approach unless you are pretty sure that a competitor is involved.

Hunches, carefully used, can be very revealing! If you have good reason to believe that the stall is based on punishment of your company, you might learn a lot by asking, "Do you feel that you have not always received fair treatment from our company?"

If the hunch is strong, play it!

TACTIC #3: Ask a direct question!

This is a variation of the "What if" question approach, but it is not quite as strong. You simply ask, "Is high inventory the only reason you are hesitant to buy?"

If the customer says, "Well, no. . . . There are other reasons. . . ." then you are on your way to finding out what those reasons are.

Whatever tactic you use, you've got to understand the problem before you can solve it. Once you know exactly what you're dealing with, target your solution right to the issue that must be resolved!

STRATEGIES FOR ACTION

How do you do that? How do you get the order that seems to be eluding you today? Every situation is different, every prospect is different, and every salesperson's approach is different. But here are some very helpful strategies for dealing with the two most common stalls.

The "Not Now" Stall

The most common stall is, "Not now!"

STRATEGY #1: Probe

The most effective strategy for dealing with the "I'll let you know," or "See me later" stall is *probe!* Ask questions that help the prospect explore his or her reasons for delaying.

STRATEGY #2: Sell, sell, sell!

If the desire is strong, but not strong enough, *go back to square one and sell, sell, sell!* Try to intensify the desire by focussing on those benefits that seem to mean the most to that particular customer. When the customer says, "Not now," that means it is not a top priority. Try to *make* it a top priority. Build value!

STRATEGY #3: Make it easier to buy now!

If something is going to change to make it more attractive later, try to find a way to take advantage of the promised event—*right now!* Sometimes it can be done by giving the customer an opportunity to buy now and pay later, to order now for later delivery.

STRATEGY #4: Create a sense of urgency to act now!

"Mrs. Smith, you know how inflation works. By ordering now, you can lock down the price and it won't be delivered until later!" Or, "Mr. Brown, I can now promise you delivery exactly when you want it, but you might have to wait for some time if you delay now!" You haven't threatened the customer, just reminded the customer of conditions that exist. The important thing is to give the customer a *reason* to act *now!*

STRATEGY #5: Make buying now more attractive!

Some salespeople save some extra ammunition for "see me later" situations. Most companies recognize the problem of stalls, and provide "pot sweeteners" to give their salespeople extra closing tools. Unfortunately, too many salespeople introduce all the sweeteners so early that they lose all their impact. Timing is the key to making "something for nothing" offers work!

STRATEGY #6: Appeal to fear, pride, desire for gain, and the desire to imitate!

When dealing with balky customers, the appeals listed above are the most common reasons they'll buy. Restate the benefits in terms of each of the four major motivations for buying. Bear down hard on the ones that seem to be strongest in your prospect.

STRATEGY #7: A desperation strategy—try shaming the customer into buying.

This one is a last ditch effort! Handled poorly, it can get you thrown out! Use it only as a last resort, but weigh all of the consequences before you pull it. It works like this: "Mrs. Jones, how can you deny your children the opportunity to grow and learn with this system?" People who are motivated strongly by pride or a desire to imitate can sometimes be swayed by this type of appeal. By toning it down considerably, you can use the shaming technique with even volatile customers.

STRATEGY #8: If all else fails, pin down a definite date and definite plan for action!

Set up a definite appointment, leave a pre-dated order blank with the customer, and set a time to pick it up. Do something to lock down a future time for action. It may not hold up, but it's better than nothing.

As you learn to adapt these eight strategies to your personality and selling situation, you will find that you can often close the customer who gives you the "not now" stall. Two very important points to remember: First, never beg for an order. It is seldom productive, often backfires, and is always demeaning! Peddlers beg, professionals sell! And second, always try to leave the door open for you, or someone else from your company, to come back!

The "Your Price Is Too High" Stall

How do you deal with the prospect who stalls by saying, "Your price is too high. . . . Get it down, and we've got a deal"? Most of what we said about closing and about handling the "not now" stall can be applied to price stalls. However, there are two very important principles to consider:

Principle #1: Occasionally you run into a customer who simply will never buy—until you cut the price! Sometimes it's an ego trip that always demands a price break. If you are looking for a long-term relationship with your clients, this is a bad person to get hooked up with. About the only way you can survive is to always state your prices high, and plan to cut them if you must.

Principle #2: The solution to the price stall seldom lies within the price itself! Usually the solution is in value, and occasionally it is in terms! If you can build enough value, and make the prospect want what you are selling, the price stall can be overcome! Even if money is a problem to a prospect, that prospect can usually be swayed by more convenient terms! The key to dealing with the price stall is to pull out every piece of tangible proof of value and interpret that proof into positive benefits keyed to the customer's strongest motivation for buying. Remember, when the prospect says the price is too high, the desire is too low. *Concentrate on building value—not cutting the price!* Peddlers and order-takers sell price; professional salespeople sell value!

I hope you haven't drawn the conclusion from this chapter that I think handling stalls is easy. It's one of the toughest parts of selling. Those who do it well deserve the title "professional salesperson," and they usually receive the rewards of personal satisfaction, financial gain, and recognition that go along with that title.

* * *

QUESTIONS FOR REVIEW

What do you do when the prospect says, "I like it, I'll buy it . . . but not today"? Or maybe it comes out, "It looks like just what we need, but your price is too high," or, "We can't afford it." Those are a special type of objection—the stall!

WHAT DOES IT MEAN?

Explain briefly the following statements:

1. "You can't fight a smokescreen with a smokescreen." _____

_____

_____

2. "When a customer stalls, the professionals consider it a challenge to do combat!" _____

_____

_____

PINNING DOWN THE REASON

From your own experience, give an example of when you used each of the tactics for pinning down the real reason for a stall.

Tactic #1: Isolate the reason for the stall by asking a "what if" question. "If we could settle the price question, would you buy today?"

YOUR EXAMPLE: _____

_____

_____

Tactic #2: Play a hunch! "Do you feel you have not always received fair treatment from our company?"

YOUR EXAMPLE: _____

_____

_____

Tactic #3: Ask a direct question! "Is high inventory the only reason you are hesitant to buy?"

YOUR EXAMPLE: _____

_____

_____

REVIEW STRATEGIES

Review the strategies for handling the "not now" stall. Put a check mark by the ones you have used successfully.

☐ *Strategy #1: Probe!* Ask questions that help the prospect explore his/her reasons for not buying now.

☐ *Strategy #2: Go back to square one and sell, sell, sell!*

☐ *Strategy #3: Make it easier to buy now!*

☐ *Strategy #4: Create a sense of urgency to act now!*

☐ *Strategy #5: Make buying now more attractive!* Offer something for nothing.

☐ *Strategy #6: Appeal to fear, pride, desire for gain, and the desire to imitate!* Restate the benefits in terms of each of the four most common reasons people buy.

☐ *Strategy #7: Try shaming the customer into buying!* Use only as a last-ditch effort!

☐ *Strategy #8: Pin down a definite date and concrete plan for action!* Do something to lock down a precise time for future action.

19.

How To Sell Against Competition

What is a competitor? A competitor is any person, product, or service which vies with you for a prospect's money. And, in most categories, there are plenty of them out there!

With the antitrust laws being what they are, there are very few "monopolies" in the world of selling. Name almost any product category or service that is attractive to a large segment of the public, or the business community, and you can almost instantly name many other companies who are out there to get the business.

A competitor is someone who stays up late at night, and gets up early in the morning, scheming and working hard to try to lure away people who buy from you. Competitors try to offer more quality for less money, better service, more convenience, higher prestige, and everything else you offer to your customers. Most of them are honorable people, who use honorable means; but all of them are trying hard to outperform you and your company, and keep you from getting business you would otherwise get.

Any salesperson who is going to become successful must learn to sell against the competition. Those who do it well often find that it is both financially rewarding and exciting. In fact, many salespeople who are very competitive by nature find that they are stimulated by competitors far more than they are by incentive programs, commission checks, and quotas set by their own companies.

STRATEGIES FOR BEATING COMPETITION

Most salespeople—at least most of those who want to stay around for a while—recognize that they are selling against other salespeople and have devised strategies aimed at beating that competition. Here are some of those winning strategies.

STRATEGY #1: Know your competition!

It is highly disconcerting to be interrupted by a customer, in the middle of a presentation, and introduced for the first time to a product you have never heard of.

Of course, you can always pass it off by saying something like: "I've never heard of them; they must be new!" But that approach can create several problems for you.

1. It makes you look bad. The customer might think he or she knows more about your business than you do. Some even get a sadistic pleasure out of making a salesperson squirm by using tantalizing claims for the products they are telling you about. Any time your customer knows more about your business than you know, your selling power is weakened.

2. If the customer is pretty well sold on the product you don't know anything about, that customer might find

your remark offensive. He or she might think you are attacking the customer for being such a "dummy" as to think a company you never heard of can produce something that would be competitive with your company.

3. Your ignorance gives the customer a convenient smokescreen to hide behind when you start to close the sale.

How To Spot Competition

The alert salesperson keeps all five senses working all the time to spot anything that even remotely resembles a competitor. Some even seek to develop a "sixth sense" which enables them to perceive the presence of competition.

"I always assume I am selling against a competitor until I know for sure that none is involved," a highly successful salesperson told me recently. "That way, I'm never caught off guard!"

Here are some pointers I've learned from some real professionals and through personal experience.

Tip #1: Listen to your customer!

Sometimes the customer will come right out and say, "I'm going to get bids on this purchase." But very often, the hints are much more subtle. A customer may say something like, "I want your best price on this," or "I need to talk to some other people before I can make a decision." Listen for any subtle hint that a competitor might be involved.

Tip #2: Watch for any "trail marks" left by a competitor!

Watch for signs of a competitor's presence: a car in the customer's parking lot, a salesperson's calling card on the receptionist's desk, door-openers a salesperson often uses, sales literature on the customer's desk—anything that would indicate a competitor has been there.

Tip #3: Ask around about competitors!

This has to be done carefully. A friendly receptionist or secretary will often say something like, "Mr. Jones has been swamped with salespeople today!" You can learn a lot by countering with a subtle question like, "Were they mainly new people, or those who call on him regularly?"

Competition in Disguise

Competition often comes in some strange disguises.

When the Cadillac Motor Division of General Motors was about to go under during the great depression, the company's new president asked the question, "Who is our competitor?" His research people came to the conclusion that the primary competitors were not other cars, but "diamonds and mink coats."

Everything your prospect says is important! For example, a furniture salesperson might find that a prospect is not weighing a furniture purchase against other stores, but against a contemplated trip to Europe.

It really gets tricky when the husband wants a trip to Europe, and the wife wants to take the available money to redo the house. But if the salesperson is not even aware that the conflict is going on, chances of swinging the sale to his or her product are greatly reduced.

Watch for competitors in disguise!

What You Should Know About Competitors

In an earlier section we said that "what you don't know about your competitors can cost you money." To be successful in selling against competition, you simply must know as much as you reasonably can ascertain about them.

I am not suggesting "industrial espionage," but I am suggesting that you cultivate a keen alertness to who your competitors are, and how they do business.

Know their products! The smart salesperson knows almost as much about what the competition is selling as about his or her own line.

Most companies in highly competitive industries design products in price brackets to keep up with what the competition is doing. For example, it is not accidental that Burger King has a "Whopper," MacDonald's has a "Big Mac," and Wendy's has a "Triple Decker."

Understanding this game is very important in selling against competitors in almost any field. A salesperson might find that a competitor has entered what appears to be a ridiculously low bid. On further investigation, that salesperson might find that the competitor has bid on a cheaper product line.

Make it your business to know what each of your direct competitors has to offer: features, prices, advantages, disadvantages, quality level, etc.

Know their methods of doing business! I said that most competitors are honorable people, but a few are not. For example, a salesman who attended a seminar I did for people who were calling on convenience markets, told of a competitive salesman who would slit the packages of other products on the shelf with a razor blade. When the store's customers would pick up a damaged package, they would return it to the shelf and pick up the competitor's product, even though it was not a well-known brand. Be alert for "sneaky" practices and "dirty pool."

Fortunately, unethical tactics are not the primary concern of most salespeople. What they are concerned with are such things as: terms and discounts competitors offer, shipping schedules and methods, service policies, warranties, and all the other intangibles that make it attractive for your customers to buy from them.

Often a small thing—like a two percent discount for payment within 10 days—can swing a sale in your direction.

Know their relationship with your customer! Sometimes you will find yourself selling, not against a competitive product, but against a unique relationship the competitor has established with your customer. For example, a purchasing agent might be paying more for a competitive product because it is sold by his brother-in-law. How you handle that will obviously be appropriate to the situation, but to simply sit through it is not very smart.

STRATEGY #2: Avoid open conflict with competitors!

A friend shared with me a very wise insight he had received from an old man. "You can fight with a skunk, and you can kill him, but when you finish, you'll smell just as he does," the old man had said. Now, I'm not implying that competitors are "skunks," but the principle is the same for any person in business. Open conflict almost always diminishes your standing with a competitor, and—more importantly—usually it hurts your standing with the customer you're fighting over.

Here are some principles that can help you avoid conflict with competitors:

Principle #1: Never knock a competitor's product or service! It might sound good to say, "They know what their stuff is worth," but snide remarks have a way of cheapening you and what you're selling.

To knock a competitor's product, when the customer has made up his mind to buy it, is to cast doubt on the judgment of the customer. If the customer interprets it that way, it is likely to be hard to get back in to see him or her.

Principle #2: Don't go to the other extreme! Some salespeople tend to bend over backwards to appear magnanimous toward a competitor. A simple statement that you respect the customer's appraisal, and that you recognize that customer's right to make any choice he or she wishes to make, is usually sufficient.

Principle #3: Focus on products and issues, not personalities! If you believe your product has been misrepresented by a competitor, don't brand that competitor a liar; just prove the facts.

Principle #4: Sell benefits to the customer, advantages of doing business, and the superiority of your company and its products and services. It's okay—even good—to build up the value of your proposition by selling its superiority. But, the poorest way to do that is by tearing down claims of the competition.

STRATEGY #3: Find out all you can about the customer's expectations of the competitor and his or her products!

By tactfully asking questions, you can learn a great deal that will make it easier for you to sell against the competition. Here are some things you might want to ascertain from the customer:

1. What does the customer know about the product or service the competitor is offering? The customer might not know about certain disadvantages. It is easier to sell against a competitor if you know what the customer knows.

2. How does the customer feel about the competitor and the products or services offered? If the customer still calls you "Mr. Brown," while calling your competitor "Charlie," that might indicate greater acceptance of the other person. Attack a product the customer strongly favors too directly, and you might get thrown out before you get started.

3. How close is the customer to making a decision? If the customer is taking you through the motions of a sales interview to simply prove to superiors that all options have been explored, that's a totally different selling situation from being in on the early explorations. Try to find out how near the buying decision is.

4. Why hasn't the customer already bought the competitive product or service? Is there some perceived drawback that you can capitalize on?

The more you know about the situation in which you are selling, the better you can plan your strategies to outsell the competition. Don't come across as preoccupied about the competition; just do a lot of listening, and learn all you can. It not only can help you deal with that immediate situation, but can give you valuable ammunition for future sales.

STRATEGY #4: Outsell the competitor!

Many times an underdog can win out in a sale simply because of superior salesmanship. And, that works the other way, too! Sometimes a salesperson, selling an inferior product, at a greater price, and offering less service, can close the sale you almost made because you are simply out-classed.

Here are some tips to help you outsell the competition:

1. Get there first and try to lock up the sale before a competitor gets the business. You simply cannot stay ahead of a salesperson who does a better job of pros-

pecting, time management, and closing sales than you do. The professional salesperson looks at every sale made by a competitor as a sale he or she lost.

2. Give a better presentation! Practice your presentation until you can outperform any competitive salesperson in your territory, and give every customer your best presentation.

3. Demonstrate! Get the customer involved in the presentation by showing, telling, and getting the customer to participate in the selling process. Try to move that customer to psychological ownership.

4. Build more value! Don't just claim that your product is superior; *prove it!* Invite comparison, use proof statements from satisfied customers, and sell the benefits that appeal most to your customer.

STRATEGY #5: Turn price into an asset!

If your price is lower, focus on the value received and the money saved. If it is higher, focus on increased benefits, lower risk, and hidden factors.

Amateurs get the wind knocked out of their sails by a discovery that the customer has been offered a lower price; but professional salespeople seek to turn price into an asset.

How do you do that? Here are some techniques that have proven to be effective:

1. "They must be leaving something out!" By focussing the question on what the competitor is leaving out, you can—with the customer's help—discover what, if anything, is being omitted that would make the competitive product less of a value to the customer. Also, you raise some questions in the customer's mind.

2. "Price is not the whole cost involved!" In the early days of photocopies, the Xerox people gained a competitive edge over all other makers of copy machines with this tactic. They focussed on the per copy cost, instead of the purchase price of the new machine. Gradually, other copier salespeople wised up and began to use the same tactic, but not before the name Xerox almost became a generic term for photocopied materials.

3. "Better quality is actually cheaper in the long run!" Whether it is actually true or not, extensive research indicates that most people believe that "you get what you pay for!" Particularly in times of financial uncertainty, people tend to avoid risk, and move up to quality.

4. Sell the intangibles! Remember the four most common reasons people buy: fear, pride, gain, and to imitate others. When you start selling such intangibles as reliability, reputation, prestige, convenience, and service, you can overcome price objections.

Remember, amateurs talk about price; professional salespeople talk about value!

STRATEGY #6: Make it easier and more pleasant to do business with your company than with your competitors!

A chemical salesman in my area once chartered an airplane to deliver a $10 bucket of paint to a customer in a remote area. Foolish? His customer called to say that a shipment had not come in on schedule, and although the delay could have been blamed on the freight company (which was in fact at fault), it didn't diminish the fact that the customer "desperately needed" the paint. That kind of service opened wider the door, and soon the salesman was selling more than $200,000 worth of chemicals to that customer each year.

The Rockefeller Corporation once conducted an extensive survey to determine why customers quit buying from their regular suppliers. They determined that 68% of the people who dropped a supplier did so because of "an attitude of indifference toward the customer by one or more persons representing the supplier."

Do you realize what that means? Lack of attentiveness to a customer's needs can cost you as much as two-thirds of your repeat business. It also means that your attitude of concern for the customer's best interest can help you lure business away from your competitors.

A commitment to be the most convenient, most pleasant, and most cooperative salesperson in your territory can go a long way toward making you rich.

STRATEGY #7: *Benefit from the sales you lose to competitors!*

When you feel you desperately need a sale, and a competitor walks away with one you thought you had sewed up, it is often hard to view it positively. However, professional salespeople learn to be good losers.

First, they always seek to leave the door open to future business. There is no place in professional selling for the attitude that says, "You'll be sorry!" or, "You're making a big mistake!"

Learn to be gracious—whether you win or lose! If you must celebrate, wait until you are a few blocks away, and then let out your yell. If you feel like grumbling, complain to your mate, your dog, or anyone but the customer.

Second, learn something from the experience. If a competitor beats you once with tactic, that's one point for him or her; but if that competitor beats you with the same tactic twice, that's two against you! Winners learn from their failures, but losers only wallow in their negative feelings.

Third, persist! Take the long view. Track the results of the competitor's product or service and stay ready to move in if the customer shows signs of dissatisfaction. If the customer offers enough potential for future business, keep going back, again and again, until you sell that customer.

HOW DO YOU SELL AGAINST COMPETITION?

Professional salespeople beat their competitors by using tested and proven strategies. They stay alert and know their competition; they avoid open conflict with competitive salespeople; they learn all they can from their customers; they outsell their competitors; they turn price into an asset; they make it easy and convenient for the customer to do business with them; and they benefit from the sales they lose to competitors.

* * *

REVIEW AND APPLICATION

No salesperson sells in a vacuum. There are always competitors around trying to lure business away from you. Here are two exercises that you can use to focus the strategies we have discussed in this chapter:

1. Analyze three sales you have lost to competition recently and determine how one of the seven strategies could have helped you salvage the sale:

- SALE LOST: _____

  REASON LOST: _____

  STRATEGY: _____

- SALE LOST: _____

  REASON LOST: _____

  STRATEGY: _____

- SALE LOST _____

  REASON LOST: _____

  STRATEGY: _____

2. List your most vigorous competitors and the predominant strategies you use to outsell them. Include direct competitors, like other companies selling similar products or services, and indirect competitors which take away money people could spend on your products and services:

COMPETITORS	PREDOMINANT STRATEGIES
_____	_____
_____	_____
_____	_____
_____	_____
_____	_____
_____	_____
_____	_____
_____	_____
_____	_____
_____	_____

20.

Wanted: Creative Salespeople

One thing that makes selling so much fun is that it provides many opportunities for you to be creative. Every day and each prospect present new opportunities for you to explore new possibilities.

Yet, so many salespeople miss out on those exciting possibilities because they get locked in on set patterns, and try to treat all customers alike. Granted, it's the easy way out. If you are fortunate, you can get a good, steady job, selling a well-accepted line of merchandise, and put in your eight hours each day doing the same thing over and over, for years on end. As long as demand for your products holds up, you can make a fairly good living without becoming too involved with your job, or your customers.

If that kind of career satisfies you, that's a choice you are free to make.

However, there are some of us who would get bored very quickly with telling the same story, to the same people, in the same way, year after year. We feel that deep yearning to "soar," to become more than we are, to rise to the height of our potential, to become creative salespeople.

But I'll let you in on a little secret: While computers, salesclerks, and catalogs are rapidly replacing mediocre salespeople, *the demand for creative salespeople is rapidly increasing.*

"Send me a salesperson who can think!" sales managers often say to me. "I've got too many peddlers, clerks and order-takers now!"

WHAT IS A CREATIVE SALESPERSON?

The creative salesperson is one who gets immersed in his or her career, who becomes involved with the needs and concerns of prospects and customers, who looks at problems as opportunities, who goes above and beyond the call of duty.

A creative salesperson is concerned with personal and career growth, with taking on new challenges, with reaching out for new opportunities, and with mobilizing all of his or her resources to obtain the highest possible goals

The peddler says, "Times are hard; nobody's buying!" The creative salesperson says, "Times are hard; I've got to find new and better ways to sell!" The salesclerk says, "We don't have that in your size!" The creative salesperson says, "Let me show you another suit that I think will look great on you!" The order-taker says, "How many do you want?" But the creative salesperson says, "Sure, we'll be glad to ship those to you right away! Are you aware of how much money you can save by taking advantage of our quantity discount?"

HOW DO YOU BECOME A CREATIVE SALESPERSON?

There's an old story about a young man who was greatly impressed with the size of J.P. Morgan's yacht. "How much does it cost to buy a ship like this?" he asked the industrialist. "If you have to ask, you can't afford it!" the famous business leader replied.

Creativity in selling is a little like that! It has more to do with an attitude than it does a simple formula. No one can tell you how to become creative in your approch to selling your customers.

Yet, there are certain clues to creativity in selling. Just as the great artists have studied the works of the masters who preceded them, the great salespeople study the creative salespeople who have gone before them. They seek to discover how those great salespeople expressed their creativity. They look for clues to creativity!

CLUES TO CREATIVITY

I have been inspired to greater creativity by studying the lives and writings of great leaders. I found that those people were constantly reaching out to become better than they were, and to reach new heights in their careers.

From their writings, I have gleaned some clues that have helped me to become more creative in my approaches to selling. Let me share some of those clues to creativity and offer suggestions as to how you can apply them to your daily selling experience.

CLUE #1: Sell ideas

Merchandise and services are only important to the customer when those things will provide definite benefits that can make that customer's life better in some tangible way.

For example, an audiovisual studio where I had some of my tapes recorded was struggling along, trying to sell filmstrips and equipment for use by large corporations. Finally, the company's president hit on an idea that opened up a whole new dimension of selling. He decided to get into the "retail sales training" business.

"Let us work with your sales managers and put together a custom-tailored film that your sales representatives can take into stores to train floor salespeople how to sell your products," he suggested to one of his large customers.

Soon, that large company bought a projector for each of its 60 sales representatives, and the first of a series of training films. Now, that customer buys about three films each year, with 60 copies each, and has established a pattern for other companies to follow. As noncompetitive companies have been added to the studio's clientele, a whole new business has been launched. The studio is doing exactly what it set out to do, but it is selling an idea, instead of films.

How Do You Sell Ideas?

Let me suggest some tips that can help you sell ideas.

1. *Seek to understand your customer's needs.* Get into your customer's business, profession, or personal life —wherever your products and services are used. Study what that customer does, and look for ways that what you are selling can make it easier, more profitable, more pleasant, or more productive for that customer. Take major problems your customer has and develop ways your products and services can be used to solve those problems. People buy from salespeople who understand their needs and problems.

2. *Help them grow.* The amateur looks for opportunities to sell more, but the professional looks for ways to help customers grow, to fulfill their dreams and desires, to become more effective at what they do. As your customers grow in what they do, they will need more and more of what you sell.

3. *Build on ideas you pick up along the way.* Most products and services have not come about by some great invention, but by taking ideas that were already in use and adapting them to new situations, or improving on them for their original uses. Stay alert for new ways of using each idea you pick up from a customer.

Of course, you will want to protect the interests of the person from whom you gained the idea. Most people are flattered when someone imitates what they are doing, but not if it weakens their competitive position or their standing.

If possible, find ways that the customer whose ideas you are building upon can gain from your use of his or her ideas. It will not only keep that person happy, but will encourage that person to give you more ideas you can use to close sales.

CLUE #2: *Turn intangibles into tangibles*

Some of the greatest benefits of most products and services we sell are hard for the customer to really appreciate because they are so intangible. The creative salesperson looks for ways to make them tangible.

The challenge of translating an intangible benefit, like pride of ownership or rugged durability, into something the customer can see and feel is one that only the most successful salespeople meet well.

"Put something into the customer's hand," is an old but very effective tactic. That's not too hard to do if you are selling tennis rackets or golf clubs; but, if your field is life insurance or investments, it might call for a lot more imagination.

For example, a woman selling newspaper ads to local stores was having little success because her prospects could not visualize the benefits of getting their names and services before the public. She drew up a sample ad for a large store that she had never been able to sell. When the store's manager saw the ad, he was so impressed he agreed to run it as a trial. It was so successful that he has become a regular customer. Now she says, "I wouldn't think of trying to sell an ad now without a sample to show the prospect."

Whatever you're selling, you'll sell more of it when you can devise ways to see, feel, taste, hear, or even smell the benefits of ownership. Believe me, any effort you put into developing tangible things to put into the hands of your prospects will pay off in big dividends. The better you become at it, the more you will sell.

Crossing the threshold of psychological ownership is a subtle, but vitally important, part of closing the sale. Anything you develop, or any precaution you take, to ensure that this happens can add significant power to your persuasion.

For example, my friend Tom Winninger, a highly successful real estate salesman and trainer, suggests that his clients make sure the present owners of a home are away at the time a prospect is invited for a tour. His reason: "A buyer cannot buy a house until he or she can take psychological possession, and psychological possession will not take place if the owner is at home during the showing!"

Find ways to make the customer experience the benefits of ownership before you attempt to close the sale!

Use Proof Statements and Examples

Look into your own experience to see what powerful tools proof statements and examples are. How many movies have you gone to see, stores have you visited, and products have you bought because they were recommended to you by a friend?

Your customers respond the same way! If you are claiming that a person will save money by buying a higher quality initially, prove it by stories of people (preferably their friends) who have done just that. If prestige is a strong benefit, tell them of some prestigious people who have bought it and are happy with it. Whatever the claim, back it up with examples and proof statements from people they know or respect.

Some of the most effective commercials I've heard and seen are those used by the Sharp Copier people. Local distributors throughout the country get happy customers to tell, before microphones and cameras, how happy they are with the products and services Sharp offers. Those happy customers have helped them sell a lot of copiers because they stand as proof that the claims of the salespeople are true.

Another variation of the proof statement is the testimonial letter. If customers say they have found your claims to be true, ask them if they will give you a letter, on their letterhead, explaining why they think it is true. You can collect such letters and use them for added ammunition in a closing situation.

There are some criteria for proof statements and examples:

1. Make sure the customer is happy. Some people will check up on your claims that a person they know is happy with what you are selling. Others will just casually mention your reference to the person in conversation. If that customer is unhappy, your use of him or her as a proof statement will actually weaken your position, instead of strengthening it.

2. It is a good idea to ask for permission to use a person's name and experience in selling others. A few people resent their names being used for "commercial" purposes. Celebrities may even sell their names and endorsements. You never want to offend cus-

tomers by trying to use them as a selling aid with a prospect.

3. Tactfully done, a request to use a person's name can be flattering. It can even open the door to asking them for the names of friends of theirs whom they would recommend you see. Some successful salespeople make it a policy to never leave a customer without at least one lead to follow up.

Use Visuals To Sell Intangibles

Professional salespeople become masters at illustrating every benefit of ownership by some visual effect. Specialty advertising has become a big business because many of the items they produce help salespeople reinforce their identity and drive home their points.

For example, business cards can be used very effectively to make people aware of what you are selling, and who you are. I read about a veneer salesman who has printed his calling card on a fancy-faced veneer.

It is one thing to tell a prospect about how much the cost of hospitalization has increased in recent years, but a sharp insurance salesperson will pull out a chart showing exactly how much that prospect could expect to pay for an extended stay in a local hospital.

The most effective visuals are those which enable the prospects to project themselves into the benefits of ownership. Those life-sized posters showing pictures of people vacationing on exotic South Seas islands help prospects to imagine themselves getting away from the pressures of life to a setting that looks like the Garden of Eden.

Visuals should be carefully prepared, should be aimed at accomplishing a very specific objective, and should be easily usable. Their goal is always to help the prospect take psychological ownership.

CLUE #3: Multiply applications

Find as many ways as you possibly can for customers to use what you are selling. The more uses a customer finds for your product, the more value it has to him or her. The greater their dependence on the product, the more business it will generate for you.

The people who sell smoking pipe filters learned long ago that they could multiply their sales by introducing their products to people who don't smoke pipes. Some innovative salespeople came up with a wide variety of uses for pipe filters in arts and crafts, and opened up a whole new market. Others sought out a wide range of industrial applications, and found a completely different market.

Let your imagination wander. Look for new applications for whatever you are selling. Look for new types of customers who might use your products or services.

For example, if you sell a man an automobile for personal use, check to see if he needs one for his business, or his wife, or a son or daughter. A bookkeeper who buys a calculator for office use might need a portable one for field use, and another one for use at home.

Don't be satisfied with only the end uses of products that the marketing people of your company have developed. Try to find other end uses. You will certainly increase your sales, and you might get a nice bonus if the idea catches on with other salespeople in your organization.

CLUE #4: Trade customers upward

Your best chance of boosting your dollar volume of sales is in trade-up selling. Even the order-taker can supply the customer who has already been sold by advertising with the cheapest product in the line, at the lowest price the company is willing to take. But, it takes a real professional to get the prospect to lift his or her sights to a better product with a higher price tag.

Salespeople who become good at trading customers upward become very valuable to their companies for one important reason—higher prices usually mean more profit. Amateurs think only of their commissions, which usually are based on volume. But professionals concern themselves with volume and profitability.

The secret to trade-up selling lies in building greater value. A bargain is a bargain only when it adequately meets the needs of the customer. That customer might focus only on the need to get out as cheaply as possible on the purchase price. But the successful salesperson learns how to build a desire in the customer for additional benefits that are available only in higher-priced items.

Of course, it is important to lift the customer's sights without knocking the lower-priced items. If you downgrade the lower-priced merchandise or service, you risk losing the sale entirely. A sale of a cheaper product or service is better than no sale at all. Sell the benefits of the lower-priced items, and the additional benefits and advantages of the higher-priced items.

Always respect the customer's decision! If your efforts to trade-up fail, and the customer decides to take the minimal purchase, reinforce that as a valid decision. Remember, the customer is always boss!

CLUE #5: Sell add-ons

Timid and uncertain salespeople are so delighted to have a minimal order that they often fold up their samples and rush out as soon as the customer says "yes." In doing so, they usually walk away from some real opportunities to build their sales volume, through add-on selling.

The best prospect for a sale is the one who has just said "yes." Most companies recognize this and provide additional items for the salesperson to add to the purchase. For example, once a man has bought a suit, the sharp salesperson shows him some shirts, ties, socks, and shoes that further enhance the pleasure of owning that suit. The principle can be carried over into almost any business.

Add-on selling is called vertical selling. It means that you increase the amount of goods and services you sell to each customer, and it carries with it two distinct advantages. First, it means that you can increase your sales volume by increasing the dollar amount of each sale. Secondly, it means that you can save time by selling more with less effort, and by seeing fewer people.

We said earlier that once a person says "yes," it is easier to set in motion a series of "yesses" than it is to get the first consent. Creative selling means that we take advantage of every "yes" the customer is willing to say.

If a customer makes a wise decision to buy our goods, let's give that customer an opportunity to make an even better decision by purchasing more from us.

CLUE #6: Follow up every sale

Have you ever noticed that sometimes when you take your new automobile in for service, the salesperson cannot be found—especially if you are having a problem! That salesperson might have stayed on your trail night and day before the sale, but quickly "splits the scene" once the contract has been signed.

What a shortsighted approach to selling!

The negative side of failing to follow up on a sale is that an unhappy customer can cost you future sales by refusing to buy from you, and by telling friends how unhappy he or she is with your product or service.

But there is a positive side to it as well—a happy customer can lead you to other customers. Most people appreciate a phone call or visit from a salesperson after a purchase because it shows that you have an interest in their concerns.

Following up on a sale to make sure that the customer got everything you promised in your sales interview is a very wise investment in your future. Service people, shipping clerks, and others in the delivery system can cost you plenty, without even trying. The only way to know if the customer is happy is to check up to find out.

Follow-up includes helping a customer resolve any problems or complaints connected with what you have sold him or her. The amateur takes the position that service is the responsibility of someone else within the company, but the professional takes the responsibility to see to it that the customer has received what he or she has paid for.

Of course, some customers are never satisfied, and are always making unrealistic demands. It is important to realize that, as a representative of the company, you have a responsibility to the company as well as the customer. Prompt response to a complaint, careful attention to details, and a positive attitude can go a long way toward resolving any conflict between your customer and your company.

The key is to focus on fixing the problem, not the blame. *The professional always sells to sell again!*

CLUE #7: Learn how to "bird dog"

Most really successful salespeople get a great deal of help from other people in developing leads for sales. Getting people to help you spot potential customers is called "bird dogging." Some salespeople call it "connecting." Whatever you call it, it works!

The key to effective "bird dogging" is to give people a reason to help you. Certainly you can count on friends to refer you to their friends, and satisfied customers are often motivated by pride of ownership to help you open doors, but it always helps to show your appreciation in tangible ways. You will surely want to be tactful in the way you do it, and you never want to put a friend or customer in an embarrassing position. But, with a little imagination, you can come up with many ways to share your gains with people who have helped you make them.

"You scratch my back, and I'll scratch yours" is an old way of expressing a very vital part of creative selling. Interconnecting with noncompeting salespeople, for example, can open many doors for you. A car salesperson can pass along leads to a clothing salesperson, or an athletic equipment salesperson by a mutual agreement. Swapping leads can be beneficial to all concerned—provided that you take care to protect your customers.

I have found that being genuinely helpful to other people not only makes me feel better about myself . . . it is good business.

CREATIVE SALESPEOPLE BUILD CAREERS

Creative salespeople look beyond meeting quotas and making sales calls; they seek to build sales careers through establishing long-term relationships and worthwhile avenues of service, through selling ideas, through expanding every opportunity to its full potential.

As they master the basics of selling, professionals move on to invest themselves in utilizing every vehicle for increasing their effectiveness.

REVIEW AND APPLICATION

How creative are you in selling? To help you set some goals in this area, we have developed the following exercise. Rate yourself on a scale of 1 to 10 on each of the statements, and set a goal for improving in each area:

1. I recognize and capitalize on every opportunity to expand my sales career and increase my effectiveness.

MY RATING: (1 2 3 4 5 6 7 8 9 10)
MY GOAL: _____

_____

2. I am motivated by a strong desire to reach my full potential as a human being and a salesperson.

MY RATING: (1 2 3 4 5 6 7 8 9 10)
MY GOAL: _____

_____

3. My superiors, my customers, and my peers respect me as a *thinking* person.

MY RATING: (1 2 3 4 5 6 7 8 9 10)
MY GOAL: _____

_____

4. I seek to understand my customers' needs and to help them grow, to build on ideas that I pick up along the way, and to sell ideas to my customers.

MY RATING: (1 2 3 4 5 6 7 8 9 10)
MY GOAL: _____

_____

5. I use proof statements, examples, and visuals very effectively to make the intangible benefits of what I'm selling tangible to my prospects.

MY RATING: (1 2 3 4 5 6 7 8 9 10)

MY GOAL: _____

_____

6. When a prospect asks for my best price on my cheapest items, I always trade that customer up to a higher quality and price level.

MY RATING: (1 2 3 4 5 6 7 8 9 10)

MY GOAL: _____

_____

7. I seek to increase my sales volume by adding as many "extras" as possible to every sale.

MY RATING: (1 2 3 4 5 6 7 8 9 10)

MY GOAL: _____

_____

8. I follow up on every sale to make sure the customer is happy and to open doors for future sales.

MY RATING: (1 2 3 4 5 6 7 8 9 10)

MY GOAL: _____

_____

9. I never leave a customer without a lead for another sale.

MY RATING: (1 2 3 4 5 6 7 8 9 10)

MY GOAL: _____

_____

10. I give as many people as possible reasons to help me in obtaining leads for sales.

MY RATING: (1 2 3 4 5 6 7 8 9 10)
MY GOAL: _____

_____

21.

Boost Your Personal Selling Power

As a professional salesperson, your greatest asset is your personal selling power—your power to persuade a substantial number of prospects to purchase your products at a profit!

Have you noticed that some people seem to have more of that personal selling power than others? They seem to be able to get other people to do the things they want them to do, and to enjoy doing it.

"I wish I could be that way," people often say to me.

"You can!" I reply, "if you are willing to study what they have done and do what they do!"

How does a person develop personal selling power? *They learn to use all they've got to get all they want out of life!* Here's how they do it.

1. Start with the assumption that personal selling power is not an innate trait—it is a developed characteristic. The people who have a lot of personal selling power didn't start out that way; they developed that power to persuade, carefully, and with much effort.

2. Recognize that people with great personal power didn't get that way overnight; they developed that power over a period of years. This is a day of "instant everything" when people want easy answers to complex questions, and great personal power with little effort.

3. Learn the power of targeted living. Make a total commitment to your sales career, to your company, to your personal goals, and to your customers. Do only what will get you what you want. Manage your time; don't let it manage you.

4. Study the pros, and practice what they do. Read good books, listen to cassettes from successful salespeople, and avail yourself of every opportunity to grow. Watch the people who are successful around you: the people in your company, the leaders in your business, and the leaders in your community. Then, seek to do exactly what they do.

5. Build all of your selling skills. Benjamin Franklin set about as a young man to become the "virtuous" person he hoped to be. To do this, he selected what he considered to be 13 cardinal virtues, and set them up as goals to be achieved. He would select one of those virtues each month, and concentrate all his energies on practicing that one virtue. When he had gone all the way through his list, he started over. He followed this pattern for the reminder of his life. I would suggest that you develop a system for building your skills, and follow that system faithfully until you have reached all of your goals.

POWER-BOOSTING TIPS

We said that people who have great personal selling power developed that power carefully, and with much effort, over a period of years. As I have studied the real professionals in the selling game, I have discovered some valuable tips that have enabled me to boost my personal selling power. I think you will find them useful.

TIP #1—Develop self-confidence!

Years ago, a national company ran a series of radio commercials featuring "the world's lowest-pressure salesman." You'd hear a timid knock on a door, then you'd hear the salesman talking to himself. "Nobody home, I hope, I hope, I hope." When a person answered the knock, he'd tremblingly ask, "You wouldn't want to buy a car, would you?" and the person would run all over the poor fellow in an effort to take the car away from him.

Anybody who has ever sold automobiles, or anything else for that matter, will tell you it doesn't work that way. People don't clamor to buy; they must be sold!

It's this simple: *Those people who become successful at selling do so because they believe they can!* They seek to become good at what they do, and stay with it until they know they are good. They develop self-confidence.

Now, let me make a distinction between self-confidence and arrogant egotism. The loud, boisterous egomaniac who is always telling everybody how good he or she is, is probably trying to convince himself or herself that it is true. The self-confident person lives with the quiet inner knowledge that he or she can do the job, and applies all that energy to making sales.

Self-confidence is based on a strong, positive self-image. It grows out of a deep awareness that you have value as a person, that you are valuable simply because you exist. If you are going to develop self-confidence, you first have to like yourself. Quit saying all those negative things about yourself, and accept yourself as the wonderful person you are!

Once you have accepted yourself as "lovable," move on to accept yourself as a capable person—a person who can do what you set out to do. Self-confidence grows with practice and preparation. Did you ever notice that you usually enjoy doing those things you do well? That's because you respect your abilities to do those things. Thus, they produce self-respect. If you would become a self-confident salesperson, prepare yourself and practice until you respect your abilities to do your job.

Look around you at some of the people you consider successful. You'll probably notice that they carry themselves in a self-confident manner. They walk with body erect, head held high, with steady steps, and with a look of determination. They speak clearly and distinctly; they laugh easily and they look you squarely in the eyes. It's obvious they like themselves and that they respect their abilities.

You probably already know this: When you walk into a customer's home or office with your shoulders drooped, your head sagging, with your eyes shifting all over the place, and when you speak in a timid and tentative manner, your customer picks up your lack of self-confidence right away. If your customer is a self-confident person, that customer takes charge of the sales interview and you are whipped before you start.

But here's a little secret: Act self-confident, and you will feel self-confident. You can act your way into feeling confident a lot easier than you can feel your way into acting confident.

If lack of self-confidence is a real problem to you, I would suggest that you take one of the many excellent courses that are available throughout the country now. Whatever it costs you, and whatever you have to do to build your self-confidence, it will be worth the price you pay.

A deep inner confidence in your abilities can do wonders for you in boosting your personal selling power.

TIP #2—Cultivate and exercise self-control!

You are in charge of your life, now! Whoever else may have taken charge of your decisions, your time, and your directions in life before cannot be held responsible for them now. That's your job!

You are your most valuable resource! Nobody can do for you what you can do for yourself! And, nothing can provide for your needs and desires as you can provide for them!

Yet, you have probably already discovered that you are your hardest resource to control. Bad attitudes creep in so silently that we don't even know they're there; habits take charge of us with incredible ease, and time slips away unnoticed.

My fellow trainer and personal friend Zig Ziglar has given us a real insight with his statement: "It's your attitude, not your aptitude, that determines your altitude!"

If you would increase your personal selling power, concentrate on goals, not on activities. Don't allow yourself to get caught in the "the hurrier I go the behinder I get" trap. Start first thing every morning by taking charge of your life, and manage every minute of every day!

Remember, desire is the key to all self-discipline! Keep clearly focussed on what you want out of life, and do only those things that will get you what you want.

Cultivate the habits that will pay off—habits like time management, territory management, and active listening.

TIP #3—Act important!

Everything about you does one of two things: it either sells, or unsells!

The way you look, your personal mannerisms, your voice, your facial expressions, your posture (while sitting or standing), your communications skills—everything about you speaks loudly and clearly to the customer!

The people who have the power to purchase your products are too busy to waste their time on anybody whom they are not convinced will have something important to say to them. Your task is to convince them, and keep them convinced, that the time they spend with you will be time well invested.

Therefore, it is very important that you look important, act important, speak as one who has something important to say to them, and present an image that commands attention.

Many of the best actors of Hollywood have utterly failed when they have tried to play roles in Broadway shows. Why? They lack that all-important ingredient—stage presence. Film producers can make up for their lack of stage presence by masterful lighting, by using flattering camera angles, by showing larger-than-life close-ups, by careful editing, and many other techniques. But, when actors step onto the stage, the audience either "feels" their presence, or it doesn't! They either bring the audience to its feet, or hear the "boos" of the crowd, depending on how good they are at projecting their images.

The sales stage is a little like that: You either project an image of importance, or you project an image of unimportance. And, the difference means either success or failure in selling.

Here are some pointers to help you boost your personal selling power through projecting an image of importance:

1. *Look your best!* People buy from salespeople who look successful. It's this simple: people back winners! You have the right to dress exactly as you please, to wear your hair as you please, and to drive any automobile you please, but your customers have the right to accept or reject you on any basis they choose. A neat, business-like appearance can open doors for you that nothing else can open.

2. *Act important!* If you come into a customer's home or place of business like an old friend dropping by—without an invitation—the customer is likely to relate to you as a pest to be gotten rid of as soon as possible. Cultivate a business-like manner. Remember, people buy from salespeople whose abilities they respect.

3. *Speak like you have something important to say!* "I was just in the neighborhood and thought I'd give you a call to see if we could possibly get together," says to your customer that what you have to say is not very important to you, or to him! Learn to express yourself as one who has something to say that is extremely important for the customer to hear. Strive to create the impression that refusing to talk to you would deprive that customer of some very valuable information —information he or she needs almost desperately to hear.

4. *Act deliberately, but not hurriedly!* Practice your demonstrations and presentations until you can make every move with the grace and style of a ballet dancer. Make every presentation a major production that says to the customer that what you are telling him or her is extremely valuable information.

5. *Respect your own time, and the customer's time!* Show up on time, get down to business as soon as you have broken the ice, finish your presentation on schedule, and terminate the interview when you have

finished. Don't waste your time, or the customer's time, by sitting around chatting. If you and the customer like each other and want to socialize, do it on the golf course, the tennis court, or some other suitable place, at a suitable time.

6. *Know what you're talking about, and talk about what you know!* If you have properly prepared, you should know what you are going to present to the customer, and how you are going to present it. Say it with words as strong as cannonballs. Use action words and focus on facts. But don't stop there; back up every claim you make with solid information, visuals, and demonstrations.

If you will learn to act important, you will be received as a Very Important Person; you can boost your personal selling power.

TIP #4—Build power through trust!

People buy from salespeople they trust!

The natural reaction of a prospect whose territory has been "invaded" by a salesperson, is to become tense, to respond with wariness to the new "intruder." Your task is to reduce the tension by creating trust within that prospect. It's a real challenge, but those salespeople who do it well develop great personal selling power.

These pointers can help you boost your power through building trust:

1. *Set the prospect's mind at ease!* A warm, friendly manner can help break down the psychological barriers the selling situation presents.

2. *Express a sincere interest in the prospect!* Get to know the prospect, and allow the prospect to get to know you. Ask nonthreatening questions that give you in-

sight into that person's motivations. Look for common ground, and assure the prospect you are there to help him or her discover something that can benefit him or her.

3. *Be truthful!* I once saw a sign that said, "All salesmen, except you and me, are liars; and sometimes I wonder about you!" It is unfortunate, but salespeople have a reputation for being untruthful. The only way to overcome that false impression is to be absolutely truthful, yourself.

4. *Be loyal!* Customers come to trust those salespeople who continually demonstrate that they have their best interests at heart. And, people buy from salespeople whose loyalty is demonstrated year after year.

5. *Be dependable!* When you make a promise, deliver on it; when you give information, make sure it's accurate; and when there is a problem, make sure the customer can depend on you to get it straightened out.

6. *Operate with complete integrity!* A few bucks saved, or made, by "sneaky" tactics can cost you a great deal of money. Sooner or later, the truth usually comes out. Make sure that when that truth surfaces, the customer respects your integrity.

If what you are selling is of such little value that you have to damage trust to sell it, you owe it to yourself and your customers to find something else to sell. Building trust can not only make your life a lot more pleasant, it can boost your personal selling power.

TIP #5—Be cheerful!

Nobody likes to be around a grumbler, or a pessimist. And, customers have the option not to stay around those people who are always spreading gloom.

"Most people are about as happy as they make up their minds to be," said Abraham Lincoln. I learned a long time ago that what the wise old statesman said is true, and I can tell you from personal experience that people have been a lot happier to see me ever since.

There are two ways to look at life: a positive way, and a negative way. The negative person says a glass is half-empty, the positive person says that glass is half-full. Both are seeing the same glass, and the same contents, but they are viewing it from different perspectives.

If you want to boost your personal selling power, put the bite on that grumbling and negative attitude. Share your joys and your victories with your customers, but keep your troubles to yourself.

TIP #6—Watch your "saleside manner!"

People speak of a doctor's human relations attitude and practices as a "bedside manner." We might then conclude that a salesperson has a "saleside manner" of dealing with other people.

We simply cannot afford to treat any of our customers, or anybody connected with them, in anything less than a courteous, respectful, and friendly manner. People who don't like you can, and usually do, stop doing business with you.

These pointers can help you maintain a good "saleside manner."

1. *Respect and treat with dignity every prospect and all those connected with him or her.* A person's secretary, or mate, or co-worker can either help you or hurt you in your efforts to make sales.

2. *Speak courteously to everyone.* A warm and cordial greeting, saying "please" and "thank you," and pay-

ing personal attention to everyone in a home or place of business can go a long way toward making you welcome each time you call.

3. *Respect every person's authority!* Of course, you want to get to the decision-makers, but don't step on someone's toes to do it. That secretary you by-pass through devious means today, might be the purchasing agent you have to see on your next trip.

4. *Seek to establish "win/win" relationships with all people.* Make sure that everyone you contact gets something out of their dealings with you—even if it is nothing more than a warm feeling from knowing you.

5. *Never allow anyone to become your enemy.* There's a wise old saying that "it takes two people to make a fight!" One thing a salesperson does not need is enemies. Try, with everything within you, to resolve the conflicts that arise during the normal course of business.

6. *Never lose a friend (or a sale) by winning an argument.* Most arguments are over trivial matters, but their cost can be astronomical. An argument is nothing more than a discussion that has gotten out of hand. The skillful salesperson learns how to put things back in perspective.

Cultivating a good "saleside manner" can help you boost your personal selling power.

TIP #7—Learn to remember!

People love it when you remember their names, important details about them, and information they consider important. Why? Because it makes them feel that they are important to you.

A good memory can help you in other ways. For example, something a prospect says during a sales interview might be very helpful to you in later calls—if you can only remember it.

The following tips can help you improve your memory, and boost your personal selling power.

1. *Pay attention!* The greatest reason most people can't remember details and names is that they are preoccupied with something else at the time of the encounter. Forget that airplane you've got to catch, that tire that's about to go flat, that unhappy customer you just left—forget everything else and concentrate entirely on the person you are with at the moment.

   Practice awareness of everything that goes on during a sales interview. Make it an experience to remember.

2. *Get names and details correctly!* If you don't understand a person's name, or something that person says, ask them to repeat it. Learning to actively listen can help you build your memory.

3. *Write down names and important details!* Writing things down not only safeguards you against lapses of memory, it helps you to remember. When you concentrate enough to put something down on paper, you are much more likely to recall it later.

4. *Read over your notes often!* Memory can be reinforced through repetition. Read your notes aloud as many times as it takes for them to sink into your memory. Throw them away only when you are sure you can remember them.

5. *Make your mind work for you!* It's easy to say, "I just can't remember names." But, the fact is that if you will train your mind to respond to your com-

mands, it will remember an amazing number of names and details.

If you really want to remember something, you can remember it. If you don't believe that, consider this scenario. Suppose I were to tell you that I'd give you a million dollars if you would remember my name for exactly one year. Would you remember it? You bet your bottom dollar you would! So you see, you can remember what you want to remember.

Now, I can't promise to give you a million dollars for remembering my name, but I can promise you this: Learn to remember names and important details and you can boost your personal selling power. You might even be able to make more than a million bucks by becoming a master at remembering.

TIP #8—Keep fit physically, emotionally, and spiritually!

Modern medical people have discovered that our bodies, our minds, and our emotions are all interconnected. Each has an impact on the other, almost constantly.

Another way of saying it is that if you want to reach your full potential of personal selling power, you must keep fit physically, emotionally, and spiritually.

Remember, we have said that you are your greatest resource; you are worth treating with the highest respect. These pointers can help you do that.

1. *Treat your body like the marvelous and intricate instrument that it is!*

   Let me ask you a question: When you make a sales call, what part of you is visible to the customer? It's your body, of course! Your physical presence is the only way your customers can experience you! Doesn't it make sense, then, to keep that most crucial ingredient of your sales career in top form?

You know all the rules of good health: plenty of rest, good diet, proper exercise, and control of habits. But, have you ever thought about how important a part your body plays in your sales career? Your ability to make sales is directly related to how well you take care of your body! If you don't believe that, think about how poorly you perform when you are suffering from a severe headache, or the "flu."

Keep your body in top form, and you can boost your personal selling power!

2. *Keep your mind and emotions in top working order!* Computers can't sell people, and people can't sell to computers. Why? Because people have minds, they have hearts, they have emotions; computers don't!

Your ability to think, to reason, to use common sense, and to care are some of the great attributes that can make you a powerful salesperson. A well-trained, alert mind is one of the most powerful forces in the world.

When you allow yourself to become mentally flabby, to fall into ruts of mental complacency, and to become scattered in your thinking, your personal selling power drops off dramatically. But when you are alert, mentally disciplined, and concentrated, you are a wonderful selling "machine."

Likewise, when you are tense, worried, anxious, or lackadaisical emotionally, you become almost impotent in selling. But when you are relaxed, feeling on top of the world, and highly motivated, the sky is your limit.

You owe it to yourself, your customers, and your company to keep fit emotionally and mentally. You can do this by constantly reading from the great books which are so widely available today, and by regularly feeding positive thoughts into your mind.

3. *Get in touch, and stay in touch, with your deep inner resources.*

Cavett Robert, who is one of America's foremost motivational speakers and one of my beloved mentors, tells a story about an event that occurred on an African safari. For three days, the native pack carriers ran through the jungle, with heavy loads, seldom pausing to rest. But, on the fourth day, these natives refused to budge.

"Why are they just sitting there?" asked the leader of the safari. "Do they want more money? Are they angry with us? What's the problem?"

"Oh, it's nothing like that," replied the hunting guide. "For three days they have run through the jungle at full speed. Today, they must wait for their souls to catch up with their bodies!"

In the mad rush of what some have called the "rat race" of selling, it is easy to lose touch with those things that really matter. It becomes absolutely crucial to take some time out to simply allow your "soul to catch up with your body."

Someone has observed that "a person should drive his ambition, not be driven by it."

TIP #9—Go the extra mile!

A very successful salesman was once asked to what he attributed his extraordinary success. "And then some," he replied.

"When I first started selling," he went on to explain, "I played a little trick on myself. No matter who I was working for, I pretended that the business was mine. I would always do everything that was expected of me—and then some!"

Those people who make it big in selling are the ones who are willing to go the extra mile, to do more than their employers expect of them. If the company expects them to make 20 calls a day, they will make 25; if the quota is set at 10 units a week, they try to sell 12; if everyone else starts work at 9:00 AM, they will hit it at 8:00 AM.

Salespeople who put power in their selling know that much of their effectiveness comes from the extra miles they put in. Perhaps that is why they are always ahead of everybody else.

Going the extra mile also means being persistent. "How many times does a customer have to say 'no' before you will accept it as final?" I once asked a group of veteran salespeople. "Five," said one of them; "Seven," said another; but one wily old pro said, "I never completely accept it!"

"Nothing will replace persistence," said President Calvin Coolidge.

If you would boost your personal selling power, be persistent.

TIP #10—Respect the feelings of others!

One of my favorite stories is about the young man who was slated to preach his first sermon, on a special Sunday. He had completed four years of college, and three years of seminary training, and his head was brimming with information he couldn't wait to get out.

That first sermon was to be preached in his home church, with his father as the pastor. All of his friends from by-gone days were on hand. He had studied most of the night before, and was ready to "lay a sermon on that crowd."

With head erect, shoulders squared, and a "know-it-all" look, he proudly strode to the pulpit. Then, he turned to face that audience. When he looked into all those expectant faces, he forgot everything he'd planned to say. After a few minutes of spouting out incoherent sentences, he humbly strolled back to his seat, shoulders sagging, head down, and eyes glued to the floor.

"Son," his wise old father told him later, "if you'd gone up more like you came down, you'd have been able to come down more like you went up."

Salespeople who are filled with product information and sales knowledge tend to approach people in a proud, almost "cocky" manner. They can't wait to put a sales pitch on a customer. But, sooner or later, they find out that other people have feelings, too. They discover that all their "cockiness" turns customers off, instead of turning them on.

It is a mark of maturity in selling to respect the feelings of others, and it's a good way to boost your personal selling power. Respect the feelings of others, and they'll respect you.

YOUR PERSONAL SELLING POWER

The measure of your personal selling power is your power to persuade many prospects to purchase your products at a profit! It takes time, commitment, study, and effort, but you can develop that tremendous personal selling power that you so much admire in other people.

You can be a very successful salesperson, if you are willing to pay the price!

* * *

REVIEW AND APPLICATION

As you review each of the 10 tips for boosting your personal selling power, set a goal for making it work for you during the next month.

1. Develop self-confidence!
MY GOAL: _____

_____

2. Cultivate and exercise self-control!
MY GOAL: _____

_____

3. Act important!
MY GOAL: _____

_____

4. Build power through trust!
MY GOAL: _____

_____

5. Be cheerful!
MY GOAL: _____

_____

6. Watch your "saleside manner!"
MY GOAL: _____

_____

7. Learn to remember!
MY GOAL: _____

_____

8. Keep fit physically, emotionally, and spiritually!
MY GOAL: _____

9. Go the extra mile!
MY GOAL: _____

10. Respect the feelings of others!
MY GOAL: _____

22.

Professional Selling: "Mind Over Matter"

The hotel coffee shop did not open early enough for my schedule one morning, so I dropped into one of those "greasy spoon" all-night restaurants for breakfast. It reminded me of "Mel's Diner," of TV fame.

"All right!" said the gum-popping waitress. "What'll it be?"

"Do you have a menu?" I asked.

"It's on the wall!" she responded with that blank stare, right out of a "Grade B" movie.

Now, I like to try to cheer up people who look bored with life, so when she threw my plate of eggs and bacon on the counter, I commented on what a beautiful morning I thought it was going to be.

"Honey," she responded, "all mornings are beautiful for sleeping!" She turned out to be quite a philosopher.

"It's been a long night, huh?" I said, determined to break through that empty stare.

"It's just a case of mind over matter. . . . If you don't mind, it don't matter!" she told me with all the enthusiasm of a patient walking in for a root canal.

"Everybody's got to be somewhere," she went on, "and this is where I gotta be!"

What a pity, I thought. Here is a person in her early thirties, who's already dead—she just hasn't been buried yet!

What a contrast from the real professional salespeople with whom I spend most of my time! They do "mind," and to them "it" really does "matter!"

As I sat there in that dingy, impersonal place, trying to eat my sloppily prepared food, and observing the robot-like people around me, I thought about some of those special salespeople who decorate my daily life.

WHAT MAKES PROFESSIONAL SALESPEOPLE SO SPECIAL?

"What makes them so special?" I pondered. Then I began to think of some of the traits that go into making a professional salesperson.

They feel good about themselves and what they're doing! They have moved past the "quiet desperation" with which Thoreau said most people live their lives. Most of them decided long ago that a life is too short to be spent doing something they didn't want to be doing, and have charted a course that will take them where they want to go.

They're self-reliant! Sure, professionals rely on other people for the help they need in closing sales, but they reciprocate by giving in return more than they receive from others. They know that ultimately they will decide how far they will go in their careers, and they want to go as far as they possibly can.

Professional salespeople are enthusiastic! You'll find them excited about life, about their work, about what they're selling, about the goals they have set for themselves—about everything that touches their lives.

They care about other people! Professionals have learned to *use things* and *value people!* They care about their families, and want to provide the best for them; they care about their customers, and want to give them the best values for the least amount of money; they care about their companies, and want to represent them with integrity and dignity.

They have the feeling that they are in control of their lives! You won't find a real professional salesperson sitting around waiting for the government to solve all their problems, or somebody to come along and give them something for nothing. They exercise discipline over themselves, their time, and their opportunities.

They're positive people! When the negative salespeople in their organization, or those who sit around motels, gather to talk about how bad business is and how hard it is to sell "nowadays," you'll see them slip out and find successful people who are talking about positive things and looking for solutions to problems.

Professional salespeople are warm and approachable! Confident in their specialized knowledge, they don't feel the necessity to impress everybody around them with all they know. They are sure enough of themselves to remain open, all the time, in hopes they may learn even more.

And, professional salespeople are reliable! You can count on them! You can trust them to come through on what they've promised to do.

COMMITMENT TO EXCELLENCE

Vince Lombardi, the legendary coach of the Green Bay Packers football team, constantly reminded his players that what separated them from the amateurs was their attitude.

Just before the biggest game most of them would ever play, the coach pointed out that there would come a time when the game would be over and the stadium empty, the television cameras would focus on other people, and they would be left alone with only their Superbowl rings and memories.

One thing will survive the passage of time, the onslaughts of criticism, the disappointments of failure, and the triumphs of victory, the coach told them. What is it that will make life matter? It is the self-respect that only grows out of "your commitment to excellence!"

LIFE'S BIGGEST QUESTION

"Have you done the very best that you could do with all the resources and opportunities you have been given?" That's the big question life asks.

It's a question only you can answer, because only you know what you could have done.

When you can answer "YES" to that question, when you're really sure that you are giving your sales career your best shot, every day of your life, you are well on your way to deserving the title *"A PROFESSIONAL SALESPERSON!"*

Index

Accountability, professional salesperson having, 14
Action time, managing, 47-48, 105
Alternate close, 188
Appearance
    in communication, 91
    importance boosted by, 257
    physical fitness improving, 263-264
Applications of product, creativity multiplying, 243
Appointments, time management requiring good, 47
Assume the sale close, 188-189
Attention, memory improved by careful, 262

Bad habits, time management guarding against, 48
Benefits, value built through selling, 165-166
Better act now close, 190
"Bird-dogging," in creative selling, 246-247
Brainpower
    (See Knowledge)
Bring your own witness close, 190-191
Buying
    desire as key to, 161-164
    reasons for, 151-152
    reasons for failure to, 152, 202-205
        (See also Selling process)

Cheerfulness, personal selling power achieved through, 259-260
Client relationships, professional salesperson maintaining, 12-13
Closings, 175-192
    alternate, 188
    asking for order approach, 180, 192
    assume the sale approach, 188-189
    awareness needed for, 177
    basics of, 180-181
    benefits of ownership experienced before, 240-242
    better act now approach, 190
    bring your own witness approach, 190-191
    characteristics of effective, 176-178
    confidence needed for, 176-177
    constant, 187
    customer filling out order approach to, 192
    customer's understanding of product or service for, 180
    effort needed for, 178-180
    key issue settled for, 180
    little decision approach, 189-190
    motivation needed for, 176
    need or desire appealed to for, 180
    on every objection, 191
    premium offer tactic for, 191
    repeating after negative customer response, 181
    small decisions made for, 180-181
    start wrapping it up approach, 189-190
    summary, 187-188, 202
    techniques, 186-193
    trial, 180-181, 187
Communication, 89-96
    importance boosted through, 257
    listening skills in, 94-95
    nonverbal, 98
    observing skills in, 95-96
    S.L.O. formula for, 91-96
    speaking skills in, 91-93
    targeting in, 93
Company, knowledge of, 70
    of products and services of, 70-72
Competition, 221-232
    concerned attitude toward customer for dealing with, 230-231
    conflict avoided with, 226-227
    customer's expectations of, 227-228
    in disguise, 224
    familiarity with, 222-226
    learning from sales lost to, 231-232
    outselling, 228-229
    price as asset in dealing with, 229-230
    sophistication of, 28
    spotting, 223-224
    strategies for dealing with, 222-232
Confidence, lack of as reason for not buying, 203
    (See also Self-confidence)
"Connecting," in creative selling, 246-247
Constant close approach, 187

Creativity, 235-247
  add-ons and, 244-245
  "bird-dogging" and, 246-247
  clues to, 237-247
  definition, 236
  following up on sales and, 245-246
  ideas sold by, 237-239
  intangibles into tangibles by, 239-243
  product applications multiplied by, 243
  trade-up selling and, 243-244
Customer
  as adversary, 170-171
  classification of, 59
  importance of, 113
  knowledge of, 73-74
  solution implemented by, 82
  targeting, 150
  (See also Buying)
Customer, changing nature of, 21-25, 113
  busy pace, 21-22
  familiarity of with selling techniques, 22
  knowledgeability, 22-23
  media-saturated nature, 24
  self-orientation, 24-25
  value-consciousness, 23-24
Customer response, 111-120
  customer's reasons for buying determining, 118-119
  decisions made by customer for, 118
  respect for salesperson for, 116-117
  trust established for, 114-116
  understanding of customer's needs and problems determining, 119-120
  (See also Questioning)

Decisions
  closing needing, 180-181, 189-190
  customer making, 117-118
  little decision close and, 189-190
Delay
  (See Stalls)
Desire
  closing appealing to, 180
  creating, 164-165
  as key to buying decision, 161-164, 203
  needs balanced with, 164-165
  persuasion building, 166-167
  (See also Selling process)
Desire-satisfaction selling, 162-164
Direct question, in stalls, 214

Effective communication
  (See Communication)
Effectiveness, 33-41
  definition, 33-34
  targeting for, 34-41
Emotional fitness, personal selling power boosted with, 264-265
Evaluation
  of handling objections, 205
  of targeting efforts, 61
Excellence, commitment to, 274

Facts, targeting, 155
Feelings, respect for boosting personal selling power, 266-267
Flexibility, time management requiring, 46, 61
Following up on sales, 245-246

Goals
  commitment to, 40-41
  immediate, 40
  intermediate-range, 40
  long-range, 40, 62-63
  personal selling power developed by achieving, 252
  setting, 38-40
  strategies planned to meet, 58-60
  targeting requiring, 36-41
  for territory, 57-58
  (See also Targeting)

Herd instinct, bring your own witness close technique appealing to, 191
Horizontal sales increase, 58
Human relations, personal selling power needing effective, 260-261
Hunches, stalls using, 214

Ideas, creativity selling, 237-239
Immediate goals, 40
Importance, personal selling power needing image of, 256-258
Industry, knowledge of, 72-73
Intangibles, creativity turning tangibles into, 239-243
Intermediate-range goals, 40

Knowledge, 67-84

Index

of competitors, 222-226
of customers, 73-74
effective use of, 84
importance achieved through, 258
of industry, 72-73
of one's company, 70
problems, needs, and opportunities spotted with, 78-80
problems solved with, 80-82
of products and services, 70-72, 80-82
of selling techniques, 68-69
solution implementation through, 82
tracking results of sales and, 83-84

Listening
competition spotted by, 223
questions followed by, 131, 133
skills, 94-95
Lists, time management requiring, 46-47
Little decision close, 189-190
Long-range goals, 40
mobilization achieving, 62-63

Management by objectives, territory managed by, 58
Manipulative selling, 106
Master closer
(See Closings)
Memory, personal selling power needing good, 261-263
Mobilization, 56-63
evaluation and, 61
long-range goals achieved through, 62-63
results of, 61-63
scheduling for, 60-61
strategies meeting goals and objectives and, 58-60
territorial goal setting and, 57-58
territory managed by objectives and, 58
Motivation, 55-56
understanding for negotiating in selling process, 169-170
(See also Mobilization)

Names, importance of remembering, 261-263
Needs
closing appealing to, 180

customer response based on understanding of, 119-120
desire balanced with in selling process, 164-165
ideas sold by understanding, 238
knowledge spotting, 78-80
lack of as reason for not buying, 203
Negotiating, selling as, 168-171
Nonmanipulative selling, 106, 118
Nonverbal communication, 98
"Not now" stall, 215

Objections, 197-206
avoiding unnecessary, 199-200
to buying, 152, 191, 202-205
closing on every, 191
evaluating handling of, 205
pinpointing real, 200-202
preparation for handling, 198-199
Objectives, strategies meeting, 58-60
(See also Goals)
Observing skills, 95-96
Opportunities, knowledge spotting, 78-80
Order
asking for, 180, 192
customer filling out as closing technique, 192

Perception, power added to persuasion by, 105-106
Persistence
personal selling power needing, 265-266
power added to persuasion with, 107-108
Personal contact, value of, 24
Personal selling power, 251-267
cheerful attitude for, 259-260
developing, 251-252
effective human relations needed for, 260-261
emotional fitness for, 264-265
image of importance needed for, 256-258
memory acuity for, 261-263
persistence needed for, 265-266
physical fitness for, 263-264
respect for feelings of others for, 266-267
self-confidence for, 253-255
self-control for, 255
trust needed for, 258-259
Personalization, power added to persuasion by, 106-107

Persuasion, power added to, 101-108
  desire built by, 166-167
  with effective sales presentation, 104-105
  with perception, 105-106
  with persistence, 107-108
  by personalization, 106-107
  with positive approach, 102-103
  with preparation, 103-104
  by probing, 106 (See also Questioning)
  prospects dealt with for, 103
  by proving statements, 107
Physical fitness, personal selling power boosted with, 264-265
Positive approach, power added to persuasion with, 102-103
Power
  (See Personal selling power; Persuasion, power added to)
Premium offer closing tactic, 191
Preparation
  for negotiation in selling process, 168-169
  objections handled with, 168-169
  power added to persuasion with, 103-104
Presentation
  (See Sales presentation)
Price
  as asset in dealing with competition, 229-230
  objection to a reason for not buying, 203-204
  stall regarding, 217-218
Probing
  (See Questioning)
Problems
  knowledge solving, 80-82
  knowledge spotting, 78-80
Procrastination, time management avoiding, 49-50
Products
  of competition, 222-226
  customer shown use of, 82
  customer understanding for closing, 180
  salesperson's knowledge of, 70-72, 80-82
Professional
  attributes of a, 8-9
  problems of, 10-11
  respect for, 9
Professional attitude, professional salesperson maintaining, 14-15

Professional salesperson
  attributes needed to become, 11-15
  commitment to excellence by, 274
  example of, 17-20
  traits, 272-274
Proof statements, benefits of ownership experienced through, 240-241
Proofs, power added to persuasion by, 107
Props
  intangibles sold through, 242-243
  sales presentation used for, 143-144
Prospect
  (See Customer)

Questioning, 125-134
  client frightened by, 128-129
  constant close approach using, 187
  dangers involved with, 128-131
  feelings reinforced by, 132
  guidelines for, 131-133
  information given with, 133
  listening after, 131, 133
  negative feelings reinforced by, 130
  open-ended at beginning of interview, 131
  power added to persuasion by, 106
  presentation developed by, 133
  problems spotted by, 80, 82
  reasons for strength of, 127-128
  sensitive, 132
  small decisions made with, 126-127
  stalls handled with, 212-214
  targeting, 132
  targeting answers to, 154-155

Respect
  customer response requiring, 116-117
  for professionals, 9
Response
  (See Customer response)

Sales
  horizontal, 58
  tracking results of, 83-84
  vertical, 58, 244-245
Sales career inferiority complex, 7-8
Sales presentation, 137-145

Index   279

advance preparation, 139-140
attention of customer for, 142
clear, distinct speech for, 142-143
enthusiasm in, 141
as exciting show, 144-145
individualizing, 113
involvement of customer in, 143
keeping it simple and making it fun (KISMIF), 137-138
knowledge in, 69
organization of for effective time management, 45-46
personalizing, 107
power added to persuasion by effective, 104-105
practicing, 140-141
props used for, 143-144
questioning developing, 133
setting for, 141-142
strategies for, 139-144
targets for, 138
"Saleside manner," personal selling power achieved by effective, 260-261
Scheduling
  strategies implementation with, 60
  for time management, 44, 45
Self-confidence, personal selling power boosted with, 253-255
Self-control, personal selling power boosted by, 255
Selling brainpower
  (See Knowledge)
Selling power
  (See Personal selling power)
Selling process, 160-172
  add-ons and, 244-245
  basics of, 161-162
  customer as adversary and, 170-171
  desire and need balanced in, 164-165
  desire in buying decision and, 161-164
  desire—satisfaction selling and, 162-164
  following up, 245-246
  as negotiating process, 168-171
  persuasion in, 166-167
  power in (See Personal selling power)
  trade-up selling and, 243-244
  value built in selling benefits in, 165-166

vertical selling and, 244-245
Selling process, changing nature of, 25-29
  competition sophistication, 28
  cost increases of, 26
  economy complexity, 28-29
  information requirements for customers, 27
  pace of life increase, 28
  professional buyers dealt with in, 27
  travel complexity, 26-27
Selling skills
  knowledge of, 68-69
  personal selling power developed by building, 252
Service
  customer shown use of, 82
  customer understanding for closing, 180
  knowledge of, 70-72, 80-82
  professional salesperson rendering, 13
Shaming technique, for stalls, 216
S.L.O. formula, for effective communication, 91-96
Speaking skills, 91-93
Specialized knowledge, professional salesperson requiring, 11-12
Stalls, 211-218
  bring your own witness close approach as, 191
  direct question for, 214
  hunches used with, 214
  "not now," 215-217
  "price too high," 217-218
  questions asked to understand reason for, 212-214
  shaming technique used for, 216
  strategies for dealing with, 215-218
  "what if" question for, 213-214
Start wrapping it up close, 189-190
Strategies
  goals and objectives met by, 58-60
  scheduling implementing, 60-61
Summary close, 187-188
  for pinpointing real objection, 202

Tangibles, creativity turning intangibles into, 239-243
Targeting, 34-41, 149-156
  answers to questions, 154-155
  of communication, 93
  customer, 150

evaluation of, 61
facts, 155
goal-setting required by, 36-41
key issue, 150-152
personal selling power developed through, 252
primary point of interest, 152-153
questions and, 132
for sales presentation, 138
timing, 153-154
(See also Goals)
Territory
goals for, 57-58
managed by objectives, 58
Testimonial letter, benefits of ownership experienced through, 241-242
Time management, 43-51
action time, 47-48, 105
bad habits avoidance, 48
in closings, 177
flexibility in, 46, 61
good appointments for, 47
importance achieved through, 257-258
importance of time, 47
money saved through effective, 50-51
organization for, 46
presentation organization, 45-46
procrastination avoidance, 49-50
scheduling, 44, 45, 60-61
targeting and, 153-154
"to do" list for, 46-47
travel and, 46
"To do" lists, time management requiring, 46-47
Tracking results, of sales, 83-84
Trade-up selling, 243-244
Traveling
complexity of, 26-27
time management during, 46
Trial closings, 180-181, 187
Trust
customer response requiring, 114-116
personal selling power achieved by establishing, 258-259

Value, selling benefits building, 165-166
Vertical selling, 244-245
increase in, 58
Visuals
(See Props)

"What if" question, stalls handled with, 213-214

For information of Mr. Qubein's speaking engagements and cassette albums, please contact *Creative Services, Inc., P.O. Box 6008, High Point, North Carolina 27262*; (919) 889-3010.

I. TECHNIQUES OF PROFESSIONAL SELLING

Here's an eight-cassette album that will help you learn all the important basics in the world of selling. This practical step-by-step guide can make you a top salesperson. Nido Qubein calls on his personal experience as a professional sales trainer and a proven, successful salesman to share with you some of his dynamic principles. Packed in a handsome, sturdy vinyl binder, this program is worth being listened to again and again by both the novice and the professional. You'll get 16 different presentations recorded on eight cassettes, including: Increase Your Effectivenesss; Build Your Sales Communications Skills; Add Power To Your Persuasion; Work Smarter—Not Just Harder; Manage Your Territory; Manage Your Opportunities; Become Your Company's Field Expert; Turn Knowledge Into Sales; Play To The Customer; Discover The Power Of Asking Questions; Focus On Maximum Effect; You Can Close With Confidence; Close Like The Pros; Turn Objections Into Sales; Turn Stalls Into Action. ($89)

II. SUCCESS SYSTEM

With this eight-cassette series, Nido Qubein can help you to awaken your sleeping giant and to excell in your career. As a top professional speaker, Nido has shared the contents of this program with hundreds of audiences around the country. And here for your personal library are the dynamic principles which lead to successful living. This cassette program is a fast-moving, hard-hitting, factual presentation designed for use by a wide variety of individuals and groups. It is practical and meaningful. In a few hours, you too can discover how to possess the magic power of successful living. You'll get 16 idea-packed sessions including: How To Enjoy A Winner's Attitude; How To Develop Self-Confidence; How To Set And Monitor Your Goals; How To Manage Your Time Effectively; How To Be An Effective Leader; How To Motivate Yourself And Others; How To Conduct Productive Meetings; How To Put Off Procrastination; How To Handle Stress And Distress; How To Avoid Burnout. ($89)